# *Divine*
# LOVE

# *Divine* LOVE

## Women Who Have It and How You Can Too

Sally Miller

NEW HOPE®
PUBLISHERS
Gospel-Centered. Missions-Driven.

BIRMINGHAM, ALABAMA

New Hope® Publishers
PO Box 12065
Birmingham, AL 35202-2065
NewHopeDigital.com
New Hope Publishers is a division of WMU®.

Library of Congress Cataloging-in-Publication Data

Miller, Sally, 1968-
  Divine love : women who have it and how you can too / by Sally Miller.
  pages cm
  ISBN 978-1-59669-415-6 (sc)
  1. Christian women — Religious life — Textbooks. 2. God
(Christianity) — Love — Textbooks. 3. Women in the Bible. 4. Christian
women — Biography. I. Title.
  BV4527.M4555 2014
  231'.6 — dc23
    2014013763

ISBN-10: 1-59669-415-7
ISBN-13: 978-1-59669-415-6

N144121 · 0914 · 3M1

*We are kept all as securely in Love*
*in woe as in weal,*
*by the Goodness of God.*
—JULIAN OF NORWICH, *Revelations of Divine Love*

# Dedication

For Emily and Emery,
Bethany, Jennifer, Elena, Charlotte, and Jillian

*You are divine daughters,*
*held in love,*
*delight of God's life!*

# Contents

# Acknowledgments

Heartfelt thanks to: Amanda Luedeke and Chip MacGregor of MacGregor Literary; Bryan (my second favorite carpenter); Ben, Ayden, and Emily; my lifelong friends Cheri, Margie, Heather, Beth, and Julie; Suzie, Cheryl, and Sue; Stacey; Andrea (Shalom!); Mom and Dad; Rob and Kristin (my sister-in-love); Billie; my church family, especially Kathleen Poach; Abbey and Abbey; Grace; and Ashley of Wheaton College who helped with Em so I could write a few mornings a week. And thanks to Yo-Yo Ma, your artfully played "Six Unaccompanied Cello Suites" by Bach companioned and inspired me every day for the year it took to write this manuscript.

Special gratitude to New Hope Publishers for bringing wings to my work.

# A Note of Love to the Reader

*God's girls are created by God, held in His circle of love even before the beginning of time, wooed, and coaxed toward* Divine Love *for our entire lives.*

Dearest Reader:

After writing several works of nonfiction, I've learned that each woman remembers, writes, and records her own story uniquely, personally, distinctly, differently. My friends — whom I've written about over the last few years — constantly remind me, "Sal, it didn't happen exactly that way."

Inevitably, I reply, "For me, it did!"

As I've researched biographical works, reference materials, online sources, and Scripture, I've been selective in the facts, stories, and ideas I've included for each of the women featured here. I've thought, *Perhaps her story went something like this. . . .*

Please keep in mind that *Divine Love* is a work of *creative nonfiction*; a hybrid of fact and fiction. Just as facts within my resources diverged, so some of my stories and the way I tell them will diverge from your rememberings of these women. That's OK. Ultimately, I've remained true to the preponderance of resources, my convictions, and to my personal perceptions of the women storied in these pages.

Of tantamount import to me is that you'll discover *your* version, slant, take on the stories of these biblical, historical, and contemporary women. God's girls have been created by God, held in His circle of love even before the beginning of time, and wooed and coaxed toward *Divine Love* for their entire lives.

I hope and pray that as you read you'll discover the threads in their lives that tie us all together into a multicolored crazy quilt of beloved women, throughout time and territory. As you follow that thread, perhaps you'll get surprised by *Divine Love* in your own story.

Searching for colors of grace, truth, and beauty in every story,

*Sally*

> *"And I pray that you, being rooted and established in love, may have power, together with all the Lord's holy people, to grasp how wide and long and high and deep is the love of Christ, and to know this love that surpasses knowledge — that you may be filled to the measure of all the fullness of God"* (EPHESIANS 3:17–19 NIV).

# Prologue

Women everywhere, every age, are looking for cosmic, mind-blowing, gentle, everyday love. We look at: bars, yacht clubs, churches, synagogues, casinos, the farmer's market, and on the Internet. Mere mortals—no matter how sensitive, intellectually stimulating, or steamy—cannot offer this kind of enigmatic, otherworldly love.

*Divine Love* shares stories of women who've experienced divine love. This crazy cacophony of chicks includes the likes of Gomer, Harriet Tubman, Julian of Norwich, Dorcas, Joan of Arc, the Woman of Endor, the Woman of Bleeding, Pocahontas, and Xiao Min.

Each chapter begins with the facts about the featured woman: name, date of birth, notables, quotables, trivia, and so on. Then, the woman's story unfolds. Sometimes in the form of a *midrash*.

*Midrash*—this storytelling tradition uses creative interpretation of Scripture, intending to fill in gaps in the story with creative answers that may tell us more about the woman—and possibly about ourselves. The result is often a creative and conversational essay that makes us question and be open to new ways of seeing ourselves and God.

Each chapter ends with reflection and action points: creative, wise, sometimes zany suggestions for action, contemplation, and book club discussion. These help us bridge the gap between the narrative and our own sacred stories.

The stories of biblical, historical, and contemporary women help us see ourselves; discover our personal stories. They can story our spiritual lives, giving us imaginative, intuitive, symbolic hooks on which to hang our spirits. They open us to the way God graces, pursues, and comforts imperfect, quirky, often stubborn—yet beautiful—women.

As we meet Jesus with the Woman of Bleeding, charge into French battles with Joan of Arc, run away with heroine Harriet Tubman, and kick up dust with a Samaritan woman in first-century Palestine, we'll recognize simple, organic, daily ways we, too, can experience *Divine Love*.

As we journey with some of God's girls, we'll enter a healing sanctuary of memories, laughter, and longing. We'll be graced into embracing our humanness, and into realizing that nothing can separate us from the divine love of God in Christ.

We'll discover that most of God's girls are more radical than religious, sassy than sanctimonious, just like many of us. In unexpected, everyday ways, we'll be shocked when this group of girlfriends helps us find the Divine Love we've always wanted.

*I ask that with both feet planted firmly on love,*
*you'll be able to take in with all followers of Jesus*
*the extravagant dimensions of Christ's love.*
*Reach out and experience the breadth! Test its length!*
*Plumb the depths! Rise to the heights!*
*Live full lives, full in the fullness of God.*
(Ephesians 3:16–19 *The Message*)

# CHAPTER 1

# Gomer Sees Herself in the Eyes of Love

## THE FACTS

NAME: Gomer

DATE OF BIRTH: c. 770 BC

DATE OF DEATH: Sometime during the eighth century BC

OTHERWISE KNOWN AS: The Wife of Adultery

🙌 SUMMARY: Gomer marries Hosea, one of the minor Old Testament prophets. In Hosea's writings, their tumultuous marriage becomes the perfect metaphor for God's relationship with Israel (and *really* with all people, including us). Like God, Hosea loves and relentlessly pursues. Gomer, like Israel, is unfaithful, fickle, easily distracted by lesser loves.

Not much is known about our gal Gomer before her marriage to the prophet. Some biblical historians believe she was a common harlot at the time of her *betrothal* (the Old Testament equivalent of an engagement). Others think she was a cultic prostitute in service of Baal. Another group of scholars — in an effort to sidestep the moral difficulty of a holy God asking one of His guys to marry a whore — claim Gomer was virginal until after she wed, and unfaithful only after the union to her hubby. Some who adhere to the latter claim go as far as claiming that Gomer and Hosea's marriage was strictly allegorical, not literal. (See the Book of Hosea.)

🌿 TRIVIA: Gomer had three children. The first child, *Jezreel* (meaning "God sows") was fathered by Hosea. The second two, a daughter and a son, had uncertain siring. In obedience to God, Hosea named the duo *Lo-Ruhama* ("no pity"), and *Lo-Ammi* ("not my people").

🌿 NOTABLE: During Gomer's lifetime, Baal worship was prevalent among Israelites in the Northern Kingdom. Baal was a Canaanite god worshipped to achieve fertility. In light of the ways Gomer wrestled with faithfulness in her marriage, it's interesting to note that, in the Old Testament, the noun *baal* means "lord, owner, possessor, or husband." The noun comes directly from a Hebrew verb meaning "to marry" or "rule over." Beyond misplaced religious devotion, in biblical times, prostitution was associated with poverty, trafficking, and more.

🌿 QUOTABLE: Don't know what he sees in me, he is spirit, he is free. And I the wife of adultery, Gomer is my name.

— MICHAEL CARD (in Gomer's voice)

---

A MAXIM OF THE STORY: *Might we think that Gomer felt she was not enough, not pretty enough, smart enough, sexy enough; for a good chunk of her life searching shady, unsanctified places for approval and acceptance that would make her feel good enough? It took Gomer, as it takes some of us, years to recognize that unconditional love sat beside her every night at the dinner table, slept in her bed. No matter what Gomer did, she couldn't get away from the gracious love of her husband, just like Israel couldn't get away from God's gracious love. God saw Israel through the eyes of His love . . . and ultimately, Hosea saw Gomer this way too.*

---

The sun, in a blaze of crimson and tangerine, spilt herself into the big blue bed of Mediterranean Sea. Her Middle Eastern job was complete, signaling that Gomer's work was about to begin. Even after years of night-work, she felt a strange power arising as most of Israel turned in to their pallets. Something seemingly undeniable or unavoidable nightly challenged the brunette to rise from her bed, stretch her body, prepare for the prowl.

The Israeli evening, alive with darkness, moon, and nocturnal activity, intensified Gomer's awareness. Fires flickered warm and orange in alleyways; homeless kids chased stray dogs, gamblers clustered on corners tossing down dice and libations. This night, like hundreds before it, brought Gomer an awakened and ironic sense of promise, possibility — and repugnance.

Standing in the middle of her tent, the young beauty removed her nightdress. With verve and grace, she drew a figure eight in the air with the bedclothes, then let them drop to the floor in a gauzy puddle. Twirling toward a tiny table, Gomer bent over to grasp a tub of expensive perfumed oil. She dipped four fingers into the container. Carefully she massaged the fragrant concoction into her neck, then in a circular motion on the rest of her body.

Smiling ruefully, Gomer imagined and owned the way her soft curvaceous figure could entice, even control men. *They'll never know what hit them,* she thought sliding into a sheer sheath dress, a half dozen silver rings and a scarf of purple and gold. Gomer drew sultry black lines on eyelids and reddened lips. As she did, her body felt powerful and elusive, yet a stirring within her soul brought feelings like those of an abandoned child. In the heat of the moment it was hard to tell if the stirring was the electricity of expectation or a monstrous hunger for approval, acceptance, and admiration.

*My bangles and sandals are all I need before leaving,* Gomer thought as she shoved twelve silver bracelets over a petite wrist. Their jangle and adornment pleased the prostitute. *Perfect!* Practically pirouetting toward her shoes, Gomer imagined all that an evening like this might achieve: *a bigger tent, a stack of silver, power, notoriety, independence, affirmation . . . won't it?*

Less than twelve hours later, after a full night's work, Gomer's tent was packed with the evening's compensation: pomegranates, oil for her lamp, jugs of freshly drawn water, woolen yarns, linens, and a towering stack of silver. She grabbed a handful of coins, sat on her pallet, and with a scant drop of barely lingering energy began to count. Halfway through the tabulation, seven pieces of silver slipped from Gomer's hand scattering like spilt water on the floor. One shekel rolled on its edge toward the empty pot of perfumed oil. *Ting,* it hit the metal lid that, in neglect, hadn't been returned to the top of its container. It reminded Gomer of the moment just after sunset when she'd prepared for her surreptitious activities. Gomer tried to bring herself back to the place of eager anticipation that wrapped her when she had applied the oil. Try as she might, she could not access those emotions again. She was empty. As used up as the oil.

Gomer didn't pick up the coins. Instead, she collapsed on her pallet. Rolling onto her left side, she felt like an old woman. Every bone and joint in her body, especially her hips, ached and pulsed with pain as hot as blue-flame. Adding insult to injury, bangles dug into her forearm. Too tired to remove them, Gomer surrendered to the idea of sleeping the day away wearing the rigid adornments. Trying to achieve a modicum of comfort, Gomer gingerly tucked gauzy nightclothes, behind her head, in the small of her back and in between her knees. As she did, she caught a glimpse of why her skin was so painful. *Ah!* The bruises on her thighs made her swear and blush and cry in a nearly silent, self-abasing child's pose.

Sun snuck in slants through cracks in the exhausted woman's tent. With furrowed brow she forcefully squinted eyes shut and covered head with clothes smelling of wine and misery. Beneath her covering, Gomer could hear mothers in nearby shelters bringing crying babies to their breasts; men kissing their families good-bye and setting off to the edges of the Mediterranean where they hoped to fill nets with the heaviness of fish. To all of them it was a bright, glorious new day. To Gomer, the sunrise was sickening.

Trying to sleep, the harlot felt questions growing somewhere beneath bruises and memories of the evening's escapades. Like surges of hormones during pregnancy, the questions nauseated. They gestated and grew: embryos in the womb of Gomer's spirit. By midmorning they felt big, begging to be born. She tried to squeeze them small, holding them, not letting them escape into the reality of the day. But, an overwhelming instinctual urge to push them out overcame her. In shouts and cries the questions burst to being, *Why do you do this to yourself? This life doesn't bring you what you want, does it? You know the pattern all too well . . . the expectations and abuses! When will you learn that what you're really looking for can't be found in a stranger's bed? If you'd admit that, then what would you do? Where would you look for love and a "fix" for your insatiable need for approval . . . to be seen and loved?*

On the first day of spring, just after sunrise, Hosea appeared at the courts of Baal, near Gomer's abode. The air was fresh and saline blowing in life and mystery from the sea. The timing was uncanny. Gomer, normally dead to the world at daybreak, was in the middle of a hiatus from harlotry. Having adjusted completely to diurnal living, she was wide awake and folding sun-dried clothes when a trio of temple gossips burst into her tent. The oldest, nosiest one—with hair as twisted and unruly as curly willow—pointed an equally twisted index finger at Gomer, "There's a man . . . a beautiful older man carrying a barrel of silver . . . and he's looking for . . . he's looking for . . . you!"

Immediately Gomer felt defensive, self-protective. She assumed the man was an ex-client. "I hope you didn't tell the man where I live." Quickly, Gomer arose, and thrashing about the tent, threw a couple pieces of fruit, some dried meat, a chunk of flat bread, and two changes of clothes into a huge sacklike bag. "If he comes any closer, tell him I've closed shop . . . indefinitely."

The gossips sucked air when, just as Gomer threw back her door-flap to make an escape from the tent and the town, the gorgeous, snowy-haired older man entered. She and the stranger stood in the entryway nearly chest to chest, nose to nose. Astounded, Gomer stumbled backward into the tent and fell to her pallet. She wanted to dive under the disheveled pile of covers or, better, slide beneath a palm tree on a hidden stretch of Mediterranean beach. Instead, she sat stone still, stunned and slightly disarmed by her split-second first impression of Hosea. His stature was tall but not proud. His clothes were clean and without pretense. His adornments were few: a small silver medallion and a gold signet ring. His unexpected allure was unavoidable.

"Gomer?" he asked looking past the gaggle of women and directly into the harlot's owlish eyes.

Despite the man's gentleness, the urge to take flight still twitched in Gomer's thigh muscles. But, something gentle and welcoming in Hosea's voice — or was it the deep brown of his eyes — drew her toward him, compelling her to answer, "Yes . . . I'm . . . I'm . . . *Gomer*." The name was difficult to say. It emerged as a globular vocal splat inducing a gag impulse as it passed over her epiglottis. Ever since she could remember, Gomer hadn't liked her name. *Why couldn't mother have given me a more comely name like Delilah or Hannah, Rachael or Ruth? A name that curls the corners of the mouth, pleases the tongue, baptizes the ear?* In the moment, her name sounded more repulsive than ever. Saying it brought the red of shame to her cheeks.

Hosea gently smiled at the reticent woman, then nodding to the old hens said, "I'd like to have a word with Gomer *alone* if you will allow me that grace." Old Gossip frenetically bobbed her head up and down, winked at Hosea and corralled her friends. In a dervish of movement, she ushered the hags outside. Hosea — wanting to protect Gomer from the ill appearance of being alone with her inside the dwelling — lifted the flap indicating that they should exit. In the fresh oceanic air, the couple watched the hens walk away disappointed, dragging sandals and skirts in the sandy soil while madly hypothesizing about the *who* and *why* of the prophet's visit.

"Would you like to sit beneath that tree?" Hosea asked, gesturing toward a nearby Linum in full blossom. Gomer demurely grinned while giving a coy nod. They walked beside each other toward the largest tree on the temple's east side. The two sat beneath fragrant blossoms that created a halo of blue above their heads. Gomer studied the flowers. Then, she studied the man. Unlike most men, he looked *at* her, not *through* her as if she were a ghost. His eyes remained fixed upon hers instead of dancing about her curvaceous body from chest to feet to hips and back (as was customary in her line of work). Gomer could feel Hosea tenderly exploring only her curls of chestnut hair, her needy eyes, and lightly freckled cheeks. It felt good, new, disarming to be seen — really seen — even if it was a bit unnerving.

"You're probably wondering who I am and why I've come to call on you," Hosea said pulling a branch laden with tiny blue flowers off the tree and handing it to Gomer.

She took the branch and twirled it between thumb and index finger, then brought it close to her nose taking in salt air and a sweet lemony-floral fragrance. "I am a little curious." Instinctively she batted dark lashes like butterflies dancing about her mini-bouquet. She inhaled the intoxicating floral fragrance again, more deeply this time.

"My name is Hosea, son of Beeri. I am a prophet of God . . ."

Before he could finish the sentence, Gomer dropped the flowers and began laughing. "A prophet? Great!" *A prostitute and a prophet*, she thought. Instantly, it seemed as if passersby were pointing, laughing, whispering about the improbable pair. She felt the hope of this encounter deflating, a flame of anger and defensiveness raging in its place. "All I need is a *prophet* telling me that if I don't . . . what's the word you guys use so often? If I don't . . ." Gomer searched the hazel-brown of Hosea's irises for the answer.

"Could the word you're looking for be . . . *repent?*" Hosea asked smiling, even laughing, and then looking down at the sandy ground.

"Yeah. That's the word, *repent,*" said Gomer. The word, blasting into the conversation, sounded as ugly and obtuse as her name had. "If you've come here to tell me to *repent*, you can save your breath . . ."

"Actually," Hosea's tone was as sweet as blossoms' scent. Its kindness slaked the angry flame within Gomer; deconstructed defensive walls. "Actually, I'm not here to ask you to *repent*. I'm here to ask you to do something even more ludicrous than that." He rubbed the palms of his hands together, then looked at the ground again.

"Are you blushing?" asked the girl leaning closer to the prophet. Hosea tucked his chin more tightly to his chest and palmed his cheeks. Gomer, enjoying a familiar place of power, playfully — almost brazenly — continued, "You're blushing! You're definitely blushing!" She laughed riantly.

The harlot felt like climbing to the top of the tree and yelling, "Look, Israel, the prophet . . . God's guy . . . come to tell me to repent, is blushing!" But, glancing at Hosea she noticed a vulnerability and devotion she'd never seen on a man's face before. The look made something small and warm grow in the pit of her stomach. The small thing prohibited her outburst. In the flash of a second, Gomer realized that this moment was as fragile and lifegiving as a dove's egg. If she wanted it to matter, she knew she had to hold it gently, carefully.

Leaning toward him and almost whispering, she said, "I'm sorry. I didn't mean to . . . I wasn't trying to embarrass . . ."

Hosea inhaled deeply and audibly. He looked at Gomer, eyebrows relaxed making his eyes look even more inviting and delicate. For a second she thought he was reaching for her hand—a taboo display of public affection—instead, his hand settled on the ground behind her. Slowly, resolutely, his shaking voice emerged, "God has asked me to come here to . . . to offer you these fifteen shekels of silver," and he reached into his pocket and produced a few shiny coins.

Now Gomer was irate! *Great,* she thought, *the guy is using money* and *God to get me in the sack!* "You're as warped as they come!" She got up and started walking away from the prophet.

"Where are you going?" he asked, perplexed and confused.

"Away from you," she said, standing with hands on hips just outside the shade of the tree.

He stood and cautiously approached Gomer saying, "Please don't go. Just hear me out, then you can leave . . . if you want to." Hosea gestured for the woman to sit in the shade again. As he did, the back of his hand brushed her forearm. An electric current (or was it something else? Spirit? Heart?) surged between the unlikely couple. Gomer pulled back, dizzied and disoriented. She wanted to be the one in control, the one who used her feminine wiles to get what she wanted. Not wanting Hosea to know his true power over her, she feigned reluctance. She plopped beneath the tree. The nervous prophet joined her.

As they sat, Gomer was surprised to feel her fight-or-flight instinct shedding like old snake skin. She was curious about this man—who in a moment had made her feel safe *and* curious—a man who openly communed with God *and* with a woman like her. Looking fixedly into the farthest spot on the horizon, Gomer tried to disguise her curiosity and attraction to the prophet. "Well, spit it out then, and make it fast. I have things to do."

"These fifteen shekels of silver along with ten bushels of barley, which will be forthcoming, are for you to give to your father, Diblaim, so that," Hosea's neck was covered with splotches of red, his breathing a bit labored, "So that you might consider becoming my betrothed."

Gomer felt confused. She continued to stare at the horizon. *Was this enigmatic stranger proposing? Had God asked one of His good guys to marry a harlot? Why? If this transaction wasn't purely sexual, maybe it was political, or even worse motivated by some kind of dogmatic religious agenda.*

"Gomer?" Hosea's now familiar voice anointed her ears, beckoning her from the hurricane of confusion. "I'm asking you to be my wife. To live with me and make a life with me. In righteousness, justice, love, compassion, and faithfulness I want to pledge myself to you." The words sounded as trustworthy and true as a stone table. The resoluteness in Hosea's voice and innocence in his countenance matched his crazy claim.

"Are you nuts? Or are you serious?" Gomer asked turning her gaze away from the horizon toward the man.

"Yes. I am serious, that is . . . and maybe a little nuts too," Hosea said looking imploringly at her. Then, with the suddenness of a sunrise he offered a grin.

"What's so funny?" she asked.

"Oh, it's nothing," said the prophet setting the coins on the ground beside Gomer and breaking out into a full-fledged scimitar smile.

"You're about to laugh. I can tell. What's going on? Do I have a piece of grape skin stuck between my teeth?"

"No," said Hosea tenderly. "I'm smiling because, it looks like it's your turn to . . ."

Gomer's voice blared with impatience, "My turn to what?"

"It looks like it's your turn to blush."

Laughter built a bridge between the prostitute and the prophet as they sat beneath the Linum tree. Though Gomer never said yes to the proposal, as she watched Hosea leave Baal's court, she knew he'd be back and she ardently hoped it'd be soon.

The Linum had long since carpeted the Israeli ground beneath it with a circle of petal-blue. Gomer watched nearly every petal fall and wondered if the naked tree would elicit her betrothed's return. It did not. She turned her attention to the moon. It waxed and waned half a dozen times. Its changes became beads on a galactic abacus, which Gomer counted, wondering when her blushing white-haired man would return. Wondering why it felt as if her hope and future rested completely in his hands.

Loneliness, habit, and ther longing led Gomer to the beds of copious strangers. Lying beside meaningless men, she looked toward heaven promising, *Once I am with Hosea, should he return for me, I will leave this life behind. I will remain faithful.* By the time the sixth lunar cycle ended, Gomer could scarcely remember the warmth of Hosea's eyes, the shape of his smile, the timbre of his voice. Hope of his return diminished.

On a particularly hot afternoon, Gomer napped in her tent, retreating from the sun and her disappointment. Old Gossip, panting and wide-eyed, woke the sleeper when she appeared at the porthole of Gomer's tent. Excitedly, she squawked, "He is here! He's here! Hosea has returned! Word has come that he has just entered the Temple gate." Gomer's heart leapt with joy *and* guilt. She sprang from bed, wrapped her head with a white scarf, slid a dozen silver bangles over her arm, and ran to meet her man.

The wedding ceremony took place in Hosea's home. His immediate family along with two witnesses gathered. Gomer felt suffocated by Hosea's bearded kinsmen (one of whom winked at her) and the women who scowled, scrutinizing the dubious union. The high and lofty language of Hebrew religious vows stung Gomer's ears; full immersion in cold water, a ritual cleansing for Jewish brides, shocked, humiliated, and humbled. At the same time it gave Gomer a secret hope. As the water wet her hair, trickled down and soaked her, she hoped — even prayed — that somehow the water would wipe away the past, ready her for a new life with God's man.

Immaculately clean and ready to retire with her husband, Gomer was led to an enormous open tent where the marriage feast was well underway. The gathering included myriad more strange and loud relatives. The food was as foreign and unfamiliar as the guests. Grapevining between two cousins who eyed her, Gomer longed for the deepest darkest part of night to descend and scatter the minions. She smiled at Hosea from across the dance floor, wishing they were alone in their marriage bed. There she could work her wiles: whispering the fulfillment of desires into his eager ears. He returned her smile and read her tired eyes as if they were a scroll.

When the moon took its highest place in the sky, Hosea cleared a path in the crowd making a way toward Gomer. When he stood close enough for his bride to feel his breath, Hosea took her hand in his and said, "I am going to prepare a place for us. I know you are tired. Don't weary of waiting. Shortly, I will return."

Sweet relief descended on Gomer's head like a crown of flowers. She had waited months for Hosea in the temple of Baal; and he proved trustworthy in his return. Surely this wait would be monumentally shorter. Crowned with Hosea's promise she willed herself to endure the boisterous, judgmental relatives for a few more hours.

Hosea was a timid, transparent, careful lover. Smitten by his innocence, Gomer found ineffable pleasure in pleasing him. Gomer was kind, selfless, and generous. For the first time in her life, she reveled in the give-and-take of physical loving. Hosea loved Gomer as a woman and friend. He saw her as more than an object, plaything, or mere means to a gratifying end. One night on their king-sized pallet he told her, "Gomer, you are flesh of my flesh, bone of my bone."

In that moment the new bride laughed, hiding her confusion over the words in dozens of kisses on her besotted's chest. Though the words confounded, Gomer didn't want or try to figure them out. Guessing that Hosea had quoted an antiquated scriptural text, she tried to rest in the beauty and mystery of the words. They satiated a place in her soul that had been empty for her entire life. In the moment they satisfied the internal gnawing that made her feel less than enough and always drove her to the streets. They made her feel like part of something bigger, something that connected her to her husband's love, to God's love.

Newly found sense of fullness led to maternal longings. While Gomer listened to her new husband snore, she imagined herself with an earth-round belly. *I wonder what it would feel like to be with child. To give birth? To be a mother?* Gomer could hardly recognize herself. *Who am I becoming?* In an instant, the memory of the ritual cleansing on her wedding day flashed. *Maybe the bath really changed me,* she considered, then fell into a deep, contented sleep.

When she awoke in the morning, Gomer snuggled up to her husband. She kissed the palm of his hand. Then, she planted a row of kisses on the inside of his arm leading to his shoulder, up his neck, then, whispered in his ear, "What do you think about becoming a father?"

Hosea gave his wife a long lovely kiss on the lips. In consent and enthusiasm he lay with his wife again. Nine months later, Gomer had the first of three children, a boy.

A lamb was slaughtered and barbecued. Bread was baked, fruit was sliced; all the relatives were invited. A priest was present. "His name will be called Jezreel," Hosea announced jubilantly at the *bris* ceremony, holding his son high in the air with two worshipfully raised hands.

Gomer loved the name as much as she loved the babe. Immediately after the priest circumcised her son, the baby began to wail. Gomer grabbed the crying infant, and began nursing him for comfort. As she watched tiny cheek muscles and lips suck and draw milk she thought about the baby's moniker. Hosea had told her, "*Jezreel,*" the name God said to him, meaning, "God sows." *A perfect name,* she considered. *This little one, sown like a seed in my body, perfectly represents all the things God is growing in me: a new life, a fresh start, love and hope, motherhood.*

The occasion — despite the presence of Hosea's relatives — was perfect. Gomer felt as if nothing could mar the moment. She burped her babe. He fell asleep on her shoulder. She inhaled his intoxicating baby scent and softness. As Jezreel snored soft infant snores, she could hear Hosea's proud voice quoting the Scriptures, *A good name is to be more desired than great riches . . . better than silver and gold.* She blew her husband a kiss from across the tent.

On a particularly quiet Sabbath afternoon Gomer's heart bounced as she watched her ruddy-skinned son, with nest of curly black hair, toddle across the land. In the wake of his tangled path, she discovered a bent native flower. Hosea had told her once that the red beauty was called a *Pheasant's Eye*. Gomer bent low and picked it.

The boy found a small hill and began to roll down it on his side. Gomer delighted in his joy and abandon. Her affection for Jezreel was massive. Motherhood agreed with the reformed prostitute. She was beginning to realize, though, that being a mom had placed daily costs on her life. And Gomer slipped into feeling as though her self had died in so many ways.

Without realizing what she was doing, Gomer began plucking off crimson Pheasant Eye petals. As each one fell to the sandy ground like a raindrop, Gomer considered the losses born in her as a mother. The first petal: death of freedom and spontaneity. The second: death of newlywed afternoons alone with Hosea. The third, fourth, and fifth: death of a lithe, alluring body, of youth, and autonomy.

In the early daze of mothering, Gomer shared some of these losses, disappointments, and exhaustions at the watering well with other new mothers. It saddened her when none of the other moms seemed to understand. *They* have *to be feeling what I'm feeling. Don't they?* she thought as she lugged full water jars home. *Maybe they're all better mothers than I am. What's wrong with me?* The ponderings were as heavy as the jugs. *I guess I'm just not good enough,* she sighed as she shuffled sandals on the well-worn path.

Gomer's feelings of inadequacy and incompletion enlarged when she thought she noticed Hosea becoming distant. Ever since Jezreel's entrance Hosea seemed to her to be been spending more time head down in his scrolls, or enraptured in prophetic dictations and debates with his scribe. Gomer wondered if the prophet was jealous of her bond with the boy or if the distance between her and her man was just a normal part of married life. Hosea's love and commitment never waned. But, their connections at the dinner table, in social circles, in private, seemed strained, strangely thinner under—in Gomer's mind—the pull of family life.

Hosea slept soundly, alone on the king-sized pallet on a clear, quiet summer night lit with waxing gibbous moon. From her corner of the tent Gomer watched the chest of her son rise and fall in a calm, asymmetrical rhythm. This week she had finally weaned the child. He seemed to sleep so much better in the wake of the detachment. The weaning process had been bittersweet but necessary—an emotional umbilical cord that had to be cut so both mother and boy could progress, grow, individuate.

Almost immediately after the child was weaned, Gomer's inner aggravations with herself and Hosea exploded into insatiable monsters. Every night, they whispered in her ear with hot condemnatory breath, *You're an inadequate mother and wife. And worse, you've lost your allure. You're dried up like the gossipy hags in Baal's temple. Finished.* The monsters drove the young mother to rise from her bed in the clear quiet, stretch her body, prepare to prowl into the loneliest part of nighttime.

Wanting to prove that she still "had it," Gomer stood crazed in the corner of the tent. She removed her nightdress. With verve and grace she drew a figure eight in the air with the bedclothes then let them drop to the floor in a gauzy puddle.

*They'll never know I was gone,* she thought, sliding into clothes, a half dozen silver rings, and a scarf of purple. Gomer drew the sultry black lines on eyelids and reddened lips from days gone by. As she did, she felt something powerful and saddening stirring within her soul. In the heat of the moment it was hard to tell if the stirring was the electricity of expectation or the monsters of shame begging for approval, acceptance, and admiration; begging to be noticed . . . to be seen.

Jezreel was oblivious running about the tent eating grapes and pita dipped in honey. Hosea, unlike his son, knew exactly where Gomer had been the night before. He recognized the aroma of incense burned at the altar of Baal that clung to her clothes. He noticed the purple scarf, tousled hair, self-loathing posture. At the breakfast table, Hosea was speechless. He broke a huge hunk of unleavened bread from the loaf and handed it graciously to his bride: an oblation.

Gomer felt nauseous taking the piece, "No thank you," she said setting it back in the wooden bowl and covering it with a floury cloth. "I'm not very hungry." Hosea's silence was suffocating. A rage-filled husband would've been better than this quiet, kind prophet. Gomer wanted to retire on her pallet, hide in it. But, she knew that leaving the family table during a meal would only add sea salt to Hosea's gaping wound. She stayed in the room, skating a fig around a plate of honey, trying to become invisible.

She successfully avoided Hosea's offerings. But, his strangely relentless, kind love and earth-brown eyes were unavoidable. Like a vise they gripped her. All at once, in the dark soil of his irises, she saw disappointment and inexorable hurt. As horrific as it all was, Hosea still looked at Gomer. He *saw* her the same way he did on their day of meeting under the Linum, on their wedding day, the day their son was born. Even in this shamed moment, Hosea saw his wife as the one God had chosen for him to love: a woman of worth and value because of His deep love.

Three seasons later, under a full moon, Gomer gave birth to a baby girl. When the labor ended, Gomer handed the baby to Hosea. As he held the infant for the first time, Hosea remembered how his son Jezreel had looked fresh from God: ruddy and laden with thick dark hair. The baby girl, with scant hair, looked nothing like the boy, nothing like Hosea. A solitary tear wiggled its way down artfully etched lines on the prophet's face. As the tear reached his chin, Gomer knew her husband's troubled thoughts that the child might be that of a stranger.

Hosea held the baby girl high in the air with worshipfully raised hands and with throat closed from grief whispered, "Her name shall be called Lo-Ruhama."

At the well, town gossips wagged their tongues about Gomer's merciless unfaithfulness. With spite and venom they discussed the meaning of her daughter's name: "I will no longer show love and forgiveness." Gomer's heart was rent. She feared that she'd muted the melody of Hosea's love. And when, two years later, she bore a son of uncertain paternity, the gossips' tongues wagged again. "The boy's name, Lo-Ammi, means, 'You are not my people,'" they laughed and sneered and turned their noses toward the heavens in judgment.

At home, despite the warning in his daughter's name, Hosea continued to extend the bread of forgiveness to Gomer each morning at breakfast. Day after day, Hosea waited, managed anger, prayed that things would change. That his wife would see all he had to offer, see the value of his love and fidelity. Almost every night she eluded him, chasing approval in the beds of strangers. It was as if there were an unscalable barrier — a fortress of self-protection — growing about the woman, preventing her from receiving her husband's offerings.

On Jezreel's twelfth birthday, the family prepared for a spectacular breakfast feast of pomegranates, oranges, salt-cured meats, and breads of every shape and kind. Gomer, accustomed to the daily dance of the morning meal, waited for Hosea to pass the hunk of warm, flat, brown bread. On this day, he did not. Instead, he waited quietly for all three children to take their places at the table. Lo-Ruhama was the last to skip absentmindedly to her spot.

All were eager to eat, mouths watering, eyes big when Hosea — in an unchecked blast of fury — stood and, with herculean strength, turned the banqueting table on its end. Fruit rolled like severed heads, juices spilled, platters shattered, meat was ruined by the grit on the floor. Hosea's heart raged with all the fire and liquid igneous of a volcano. He did not look at Gomer. Instead with dark eyes iced in blue rims, he stared down and shared the prophecy: "Contend with her. She is living in sin!"

Gomer bent her head. Lo-Ruhama began to cry. She ran to Gomer and buried her shaking head in her mother's lap. The crying child did not slake Hosea's words. The prophet continued with strongly spoken words from God, "I will have no compassion on your siblings Lo-Ammi and Lo-Ruhama because they are children of your adulterous mother . . . and then she will remember how good life was." Lo-Ammi hid in a tight ball behind the overturned table and tried to hold in tears.

Jezreel, head slightly bowed, slowly approached his father. "Father . . ."

Hosea's voice became soft, steady, and resolute, "If she will stop her harlotry, I will show mercy and . . ." Hosea's tears finished the sentence. And he left the tent.

The prophecy—and Hosea's forgiveness and the sadness—kept Gomer in check for six months. On the seventh, she relapsed. This time it was worse.

Too old and used up to go it on her own, Gomer was forced to move in with a seller of women who had the largest tent (and the most concubines) at the courts of Baal. Some days Gomer felt lonely and began wondering how the prophet and her three children were doing. Most of the time she was so numb from wine, abuse, and sleep deprivation that her family seemed more like an apparition than a reality.

Even though Gomer was way past the prime for prostitutes in Baal's temple, she was a pet acquisition of the seller. He'd watched her work for years and reveled in adding her to his spoils. As his favorite, he gloried in telling her saccharine sweet lies about her place in history, the wealth he'd accrue for her. Behind her back, he stole her silver and defamed her name.

On a spring morning the seller lay beside Gomer on a large pallet, Old Gossip appeared panting at the tent porthole. She pushed her way through a herd of women.

"A delivery is here for you. It is enormous . . . grand. At least ten bushels of barley. It looks as if *someone* is trying to gift you."

The seller of women waffled between greed and his bizarre obsession with Gomer, "Bring in the spoils," he commanded in a weasel's nasal voice.

Five servants carried in enormous bags overflowing with barley. Gomer noticed Hebrew writing on the bags. It was a bold, straight hand, which she recognized but could not place. Embarrassed by her illiteracy, but pressed by curiosity, she whispered to the seller, "What is written on the bags?"

The seller, walking a circuitous path amongst the spoils said, "They're labeled with a bunch of nonsense: *righteousness, justice, love, compassion, faithfulness.* Surely someone is trying to convict me of my . . . wrongdoings . . ." Then, to the servants, "Take these bags away!"

"I don't think the message is meant for you!" Gomer uttered to her owner as she ran from his tent. Savagely escaping, she dashed through the temple courts and at the edge of the property began searching for the Linum tree. Out of breath and energy she saw it. Branches splayed, full with bright blue blossoms, the tree looked as if it held arms open, beckoning. Gomer ran to its shade and instinctively picked an aromatic branch. In the inviting shade, she recounted the words written on the bags of barley: *righteousness, justice, love* . . . They were the exact words Hosea pledged when he asked her to marry him under this very tree. Gomer twirled the branch between her thumb and index finger. She couldn't wait to give it to Hosea: a peace offering, an apology, a pledge to try to receive his love . . . again . . . and live a life of faithfulness.

At home, Gomer found Hosea studying. He looked up from his scrolls, aghast, eyes bright, pupils dilated with hope and surprise. Gomer handed him the branch. He took it. A litany of apologies and tears begged to be freed. Instead, Gomer humbly leaned toward the scrolls. "What are you studying?" she asked, her voice a long shaky line.

Hosea wanted to say, *Where have you been? Why did it take you so long to come home?* Instead he simply answered her question, "I am searching the Scriptures for an important word."

She longed to embrace the man, whisper I love yous in his ear. "Searching?" she asked, holding back. "For what?"

"I'm meditating on the definition of a Hebrew word . . ." Tears formed in the corners of Hosea's eyes. He wanted to ask Gomer if she was going to stay with him, mother their children. "Which I then search for in the Scriptures and enhance my understanding of its meaning based on how it's used in the text."

Gomer was afraid to ask, *What word are you studying?* Lest he answer: *anger, revenge, punishment, damnation.* She asked anyway, "What word are you studying, Hosea?"

"*Gomer*," he replied with a soothing warm voice.

"What?" she asked, incredulous.

"Gomer," he said again. "I'm studying the word *Gomer*."

She laughed a little and, taking a risk, put her hand on his shoulder, "I don't think my name is in the Scriptures."

"It is, and the definition is."

Fear and expectation danced within Gomer. "What does my name mean?"

The corners of Hosea's eyes crinkled with his slight smile, "Don't you know?"

"Of course not . . . or I wouldn't be asking you." Gomer felt the edges of her heart softening under the comfort of a familiar playfulness, a familial connectedness. It urged and tempted her to kiss his neck, his bicep, his chest. She resisted.

Hosea reached muscular arms above his head and before she could stop him, he pulled his wife into his lap. As she collapsed into him, her walls collapsed. With the brilliant sparkle of his brown eyes Hosea held his wife's gaze, Your name means 'complete,' Gomer. You, my beloved wife are completed by divine love. Maybe it has been hard for you to believe it, but you are finished wandering . . . *that is over!*

"Through the eyes of my love . . . really, through the eyes of God, who loves you infinitely more than I do . . . you are made complete. What you bring to the table, the bed, our children, our home . . . is enough. *You are more than enough for me.* I love you, Gomer. No matter what, I will speak kindly to you. I will allure you; and betroth you to me forever. Yes, you will stay with me, only me, and I will betroth you to me in *righteousness* and in *justice.*"

Gomer warmed and relaxed fully in the embrace of her man and in the words he spoke. She kissed him and for the first time in her life, she felt completely seen and known, and loved, nonetheless. It was a liberating, enlarging feeling as if her soul had taken flight like a soaring bird.

Until Gomer was an old, old woman, she stayed with Hosea and their three children. Through the years she learned to live in the fullness of her name. She was never perfect. But, with the grace of Hosea's steadfast love and the way He truly saw and loved her, she received the gift of God's faithful love. As she became more secure in her name, two of her children received new, real, perfect, healing nicknames. *Lo* was dropped from Lo-Ruhama's name, and she became *Ruhama*, or "loved." In kind, Lo-Ammi became *Ammi,* "my people, sons of God!"

Gomer and Hosea grew old together, watching their children and their children's children have children. Hosea never lost the twinkle in his eye for Gomer. And because she was seen and loved — year after year — Gomer was finally able to see herself and realize that she was complete because of God's divine love. Her knowing wasn't merely a heightened self-esteem. It wasn't even totally about the love of a good man, a prophet. It was more about realizing that being held in Hosea's embrace was a mere picture of the perfect, endless embrace of God: the beginning and completion of her whole self.

> *I will call them "my people" who are not my people; and I will call her "my loved one" who is not my loved one* (ROMANS 9:25 NIV).

PONDERINGS FOR THE HEART:
*Reflecting on God's Love*

Monsters of unworthiness and insufficiency, and possibly an inability to see herself as beloved, drove Gomer to unfaithfulness for most of her marriage. Israel's unfaithfulness to Yahweh was due to selfishness leading to idolatry; Gomer and Hosea are a living parable for the same. These stories are lessons to each of us in our love affair with the divine God!

It was only when Gomer could see herself through the eyes of Hosea's love (a representative of God's unconditional love) that she could begin to love herself and become open to receive lifelong love in the marriage, which brought her healing and redemption.

1. Is there anyone in your life who has seen you and truly, fully loved you? A parent? A close friend? A spouse? How is this love a mirror, for you, of God's love? And how can you be more gentle and gracious with yourself as you live into a fuller awareness of this kind of love; a love that knows all of your idiosyncrasies, shortcomings, failings, and quirks . . . and loves you — not in spite of them — but because of them?

2. Read the following as a word to you from God:

> "But down the road the population of Israel is going to explode past counting, like sand on the ocean beaches. In the very place where they were once named Nobody, they will be named God's Somebody. Everybody in Judah and everybody in Israel will be assembled as one people. They'll choose a single leader. There'll be no stopping them — a great day in Jezreel!"
>
> "Rename your brothers 'God's Somebody.'
> Rename your sisters 'All Mercy'"
>
> (HOSEA 1:10 TO 2:1 *The Message*).

Consider names you've been given in love and in fun and in times of conflict. List these. Then, list names that mean *God's Somebody* and *All Mercy,* to you.

3. Check out the Old Testament Book of Hosea, especially chapters 1–3. While you're reading, consider listening to a Michael Card cut titled, *Song of Gomer:* How do you feel as you read or listen? Why?

4. It is easy to love the "good" parts of ourselves: our hospitality and kindness and playfulness and smarts. But, what about qualities like impulsivity, overprotectiveness, passion, a penchant for anger? Can you imagine ways of seeing these qualities in the light of love? How? Is it possible to embrace and integrate the shadow sides of our humanity? Consider ways you might go about this. Talk it over with a good and trusted friend.

# HEARTBEATS:
## *Acting on God's Love*

1. One of my friends from graduate school has a word tattooed on her left wrist. The word is: *enough*. What word have you possibly written on a part of your body? Is there a word of meaning that you could "write" on your heart? Consider choosing a typeface, printing that word with enlarged letters, then printing it out and displaying it where you will see it every day. Words to consider: *enough, beloved, accepted, cherished, seen, beautiful, wonderful, worthy, valuable, complete.*

2. On a large piece of paper, draw the eyes of people closest to you. Around each eye list qualities each of these eyes recognize and love about you.

3. Think of someone who does not see herself in the eyes of love. Creatively, find a way to show her the way God beholds her, such as through a note, a phone message, an invitation to breakfast or coffee, an unexpected gift.

# CHAPTER 2

# The Woman of Bleeding Reaches Out

## THE FACTS

NAME: The Woman with the Issue of Bleeding (We'll call her Maddie.)

DATE OF BIRTH: Sometime during the first century (We'll say June 23, 7 BC.)

DATE OF DEATH: Sometime during the first century (We'll say November 11, AD 53.)

OTHERWISE KNOWN AS: The Unclean Woman

SUMMARY: Maddie dealt with a chronic issue of bleeding. The issue, coupled with strict Levitical laws concerning *ceremonial cleanliness*, caused Maddie to be a social pariah, isolated. She saw an endless string of doctors, who couldn't remediate the problem. With nowhere else to turn, Maddie reached out to a rabbi, Jesus, who was known to have healing powers. (See Mark 5:25–34.)

TRIVIA: In the first century, Jewish women were declared *ceremonially unclean* any time they menstruated. Anything they sat on or touched was unclean. They couldn't touch plates or beds, friends, or even their own husbands. Hugging a girlfriend was prohibited. Sex was unimaginable. Anything even brushed by a menstruating woman was *unclean* until it was completely scrubbed down (even then it remained *unclean* until sundown). Every month at the end of her period, a woman had to bathe, wait eight days, and then sacrifice two doves at the temple in order to be clean again.

*✑* NOTABLE: With the forthrightness that is characteristic of gospel writer Mark, he says "[Maddie] had suffered a great deal under the care of many doctors." In fact, at times their . . . repulsive or painful remedies . . . were worse than her sickness.

— ANN SPANGLER AND JEAN E. SYSWERDA

*✑* QUOTABLE: "If only I touch his [Jesus'] cloak, I will be healed." (See also Matthew 9:20–22)

A MAXIM OF THE STORY: *Maddie ignored the convention of her day in order to reach out for help, hope, and healing in an unexpected place. We can do the same!*

This was run-of-the-mill for her; Maddie had cramping, bloating, and howl-at-the-moon irritability followed by a four-day flow. On the fourth day, she began purification preparations in line with the Levitical law she and her clan embraced. *What a chore,* she thought as she laid out basin, towel, herbs, and sea salts for the next day's bathing ritual.

Her newlywed husband, Jacob, entered the courtyard, his dark hair a tangled nest of ebony curls, his bare arms lithe and inviting. He was on his way to their grove.

Her heart's desire was to drape arms 'round her man's broad neck and cover his whiskered face with kisses. If she touched him, Maddie knew he'd be considered unclean too. So, instead, she merely blew a wisp of a kiss. He caught it. Then, he lunged at her in fun. She dodged his advance by scant a handbreadth. Then, he chased her around the shelter like a child on the playground. She giggled while offering feigned protestation.

"I'm waiting for you," Jacob whispered so close she could smell his familiar saline scent. She smiled and they laughed together in the still of the day. It had been seven cycles since they'd wed. She had secretly hoped this one would bring a son.

Maddie watched her strong, gentle farmer disappear into the grove. When he was a dot in the distance, she placed seven stones on a portion of fence surrounding their property. Each day, following tomorrow's bath, she'd chuck one into the field. When the fence was bare, she'd sacrifice two doves at the temple and, then, be ready for reunion with her guy.

She hated the ritualistic cleansings. The worst part was the sojourn to the temple market. There, she'd spend a fistful of denarii on two spotless doves. The birds would coo, look imploringly at Maddie from their tiny cage. She would feel inclined to feed them, name them, and fantasize about freeing them. She always imagined what a gift it'd be to watch them soar into the Palestinian blue.

Every time Maddie was forced to make an avian sacrifice, a mental chart — replete with pros and cons of releasing the birds — would bloom in her brain. Pro: *the birds will be free.* Con: *I will remain unclean from my period.* Pro: *I won't feel bad about killing the innocent creatures.* Con: *I won't be able to sit or lie down anywhere without contaminating something.* Pro: *I can't think of another pro. Please God, give me another pro. You're the one who makes women bleed, cycling with the moon. Please, help me think of another pro.* Con: *I won't be able to make pottery, hold the hand of a friend, feed our goats, pass a plate at dinner, accidentally brush someone at the market, be close to Jacob . . .* The intellectual inventory always led to the same conclusion. The birds had to die.

As she had for as many months as Maddie could remember, she would bow her head dutifully and offer the doves to the priest. At the solid entrance of the Temple, she would not offer eye contact. He would sacrifice one of the birds as a sin offering, the other he'd set ablaze in a smoky oblation. When Maddie left the Temple she would catch a putrid whiff of burning flesh. Her body would be considered clean, but her spirit would feel as charred as the doves.

Seven days passed; the fence was devoid of stones. But, still, Maddie bled. She began a reverse-stone strategy, putting one stone on the fence for each day of bloody discharge. One rock, two rocks, three, four. *What is wrong with me?* Five, six, seven, eight, nine, ten, eleven.

"Why haven't you gone to the temple?" her husband asked on day twelve.

*I feel weak, exhausted, worried.* Thirteen, fourteen, fifteen . . . twenty . . . twenty-five, thirty . . . fifty. The farmer was getting worried, too, and frustrated and impatient. Jacob didn't mean to, but he—in his helplessness and fear and humanity—began to eye other women. She noticed. She felt fearful for herself, for him, for their marriage covenant. She started staying home all day, sleeping a lot, wondering what she could do to stop any unwelcomed guests.

Then, she'd wonder what she'd done to bring on this difficulty. *Am I being cursed for my sins? Has something inside of me gone terribly wrong? Is God punishing me for that afternoon under the fig tree with Jake before we were married? For lying? For being envious? For being ungrateful for all I've been given? Could I be dying?*

Rocks sat like nefarious and silent frogs on every inch of the fence: five years of bleeding.

"I think you should see a doctor," her devastated farmer said one Sabbath.

For the next seven years Maddie spent all she had on doctors. At least once every month, she was forced to describe the embarrassing medical symptoms to a new, potentially promising stranger. She spent hours in denigrating examinations, vulnerable and exposed. The best of medical practitioners and homeopaths couldn't agree on the genesis of her bleeding. The list of possible causes grew like a storm front in spring. Modern diagnoses of fibroid tumors, chronic menstrual disorder, a hormone imbalance, uterine hemorrhage, STD, infection, endometriosis, menorrhagia, or hemophilia were unavailable. Archaic treatments were often repulsive, even painful. They depleted Maddie of wealth and strength and hope. Hope for a child. Hope to hold on to her marriage. Hope to be creative and free and alive in any meaningful way. The treatments, along with the illness itself, erased her voluptuous curves, replacing them with bones dressed in anemic, ill-fitting skin.

Every now and then, there'd be a breakthrough. Bleeding would recede for a few glorious days. Maddie would dance and sing, lay out towels and salts and perfumes. Her husband would begin whistling in the orchards again. Suddenly, out of that Palestinian blue, she'd start feeling tired, grouchy, even forlorn, and the red reason for the anguish would return more ferociously than before.

Apart from the bleeding, Maddie was beginning to forget who she was. The pain, untidiness, and odor were beginning to define her. She couldn't remember what it was like to sit anywhere she pleased, walk freely in the village, not worry about carrying a bag full of cotton rags and perfumes. Friends stopped visiting. Her parents disowned her. She became a cursed social pariah. People looked *through*, not *at* her. Some days she wondered if she were invisible.

Worse than all of that was the realization that — most likely — her marriage was over. Though her husband still loved her, and he steadfastly offered occasional necessary graces: picnics in the orchard, walks at twilight, whispered promises of commitment . . . Maddie still noticed the ineffable sadness and desperation in his eyes. Others suggested that it was only a matter of time before he would quietly and respectfully abandon her. His sadness rent her heart almost more than her predicament. The counterfeit solace came when Maddie allowed herself to entertain thoughts of suicide for a few moments each night before sleep.

It was spring, the twelfth year of Maddie's bleeding. Chartreuse burst from the tips of every branch. Each morning songbirds, harbingers of new life, sang the promise of dawn. But, Maddie felt as if she were stuck in winter with a mere mustard seed buried beneath avalanches of snow.

She wouldn't have noticed the seed if it hadn't been for her farmer. He'd heard two women whispering outside the Temple. They clucked about a roaming rabbi and his twelve friends, including some stinky fishermen. Word had it that the troupe was wandering around Galilee, telling stories, gathering crowds, randomly healing people. Some blind could see, deaf could hear, lame could walk, lepers were healed, and word had it that dead were literally raised to life again!

"No one else has been able to help you, Mads. Maybe you should go see the curious rabbi."

In the cool of an April morning, Maddie packed a small bag (holding mostly cotton rags to conceal her messy condition). Jacob slept as she left the house. She didn't even consider a kiss. It'd been more than a decade since they'd touched or shared the same bed. She didn't even tell him where she was going. Speaking of this last seed of hope felt like it might jinx her chance of help and healing . . . of hope.

It was a twelve-hour walk to Galilee. The sojourn would definitely exacerbate her condition, perhaps to the point of death. Maddie didn't care. Still, fears pecked her mind like crows at corn. *You're chasing the wind, Maddie. This guy is probably a lunatic or liar. How could he help you when trained midwives and doctors have been stumped by your chronic condition? Even if you wind up in Galilee, you may not be able to find this guy . . . this . . . rabbi. And, if you do, who's to say he'll care about helping you?*

Heat exhaustion and waves of nausea were her walking partners. At a particularly rugged, prickly part of the path she wanted to stop. But, something beyond herself urged her forward. It seemed to say, *Just find him, then reach out to him, and all will be well.* It beckoned Maddie to take each step in the dusty road with a resolution and determination that bordered on madness.

After hiking nonstop all day, Maddie reached the summit of a hill overlooking a lake. Waves sparkled and jived with flecks of evening sun. For the first time all day, she sat down. Grass tickled her ankles — for the first time in months, she felt a flicker of anticipatory joy. Noticing the soaking wet cloths beneath her skirt diminished the pleasure of it. But, she breathed and took one last gulp of water.

Suddenly she noticed a large crowd moving, amoeba-like in the valley. The crowd nestled exactly where four patches of field adjoined. One was green. Two were a shade of gold. The fourth was crimson. Maddie figured the green field was an olive grove. The golden was grain. The red was some kind of fruit patch. *The bright-yellow must be mustard,* she whispered to herself. In that instant, something inside Maddie leapt and flickered again. It was a miniscule flutter of movement that felt like a monumental growing of hope.

From the distance, the swarm of people looked like a knot tying the four pieces of colorful field together in quilted creation. The vision was pure beauty. She noticed it. Memorized it. Held it like the baby she'd desired for years.

After changing her rags, Maddie walked down her hill toward the hubbub. Halfway down, she could see the epicenter of the commotion: the homeless rabbi and his stinky friends. *There he is! He looks a lot younger, gentler . . . more reachable than I had imagined.* She watched for a while as he played around with a company of kids. It looked as if they were playing leapfrog or some amalgam of it. He laughed and ran. So did the children. *He looks disarming and approachable enough,* she considered.

Reaching the crowd, adrenaline began to pulse through Maddie's veins. She could feel it mixing, mingling with the unclean blood. It drove her forward. With a crazed tenacity and persistence, she pushed through the amoebic crowd. With such a mass and clamor of people she had to elbow her way toward the rabbi. Each time she came in contact with someone, she shivered with worry about her contaminating touch. In her mind Maddie made a list of the strangers she'd secretly offended: *the man with the long beard and phylacteries, the boy with the crusty nose, the crippled mother of three, the beggar, the soldier, the statesman, the prostitute . . . Forgive me, God! Forgive. Me.*

Maddie was less than a dozen cubits from the rabbi. He was telling a story. She thought it rude to interrupt the tale, so she pensively, nervously waited. Suddenly an out-of-breath man, dressed in royal garb, burst toward the storyteller. Maddie heard someone from the throng call the interrupter Jairus. He fell to the ground and began pleading, "My twelve-year-old daughter is dying. Please come and put your hands on her so that she will be healed and live."

The rabbi didn't hesitate. He followed the man. As he did the large crowd followed, too, pressing in. *I have to get to him,* Maddie thought. *I can't let him get out of my sight or I may lose him.* She tried to push her way through the crowd, but was carried, as if in a tsunami, away from the healer. Sweat pooled on Maddie's brow and beneath her arms. It dripped down her chest and neck. Her frail body was wearing out. Her feet were caked with the russet-colored Galilean dust. Her hair hung in matted clumps, resembling dreadlocks, on the sides and back of her head. She felt disheveled, embarrassed, motley, unworthy, used-up, in one simple word: *unclean.*

*If I can just touch His clothes, I'll be healed,* Maddie thought as she used one last burst of strength to near the rabbi. She came up behind him. And just as she was going to tap his shoulder someone pushed her to the ground. Someone else stepped in the middle of her back. The force of it was nearly paralyzing. She struggled to stand. Barely on her knees, she noticed an azure border of tassels around the bottom of the rabbi's cloak. The tassels blew in the breeze like tiny blue bells. The moment began moving in slow motion: The rabbi took a step; the tassels wagged. Maddie crawled and reached . . . the rabbi stepped again. Maddie reached again, contaminating more people in the crowd. She reached with every fiber and will and iota of strength and energy until her index finger brushed—merely brushed—the end of one of the tassels.

Mystical, earth-shattering shivers pulsed through Maddie's spine, arms, legs, spirit. Synapses in her brain surged with the smell of home, the sight of her husband, the sound of relief, the taste of mercy. Immediately her bleeding stopped and she felt in her body that she was freed from suffering.

The Rabbi stopped. He turned in a circle. Realizing something of divine love had happened, He asked the crowd, "Who touched My clothes?"

Maddie cowered. She was in a ball before the sandaled feet of the Teacher. Somehow, because of the mystery that passed between them, she knew He knew her story. Without hearing her all too familiar doctor's office chronicle, He knew all the denigrating details of her disease. She felt sick with embarrassment and shame. She anticipated condemnation, attack, scorn, and ridicule for touching Him, contaminating Him. She trembled like a lost child.

He looked down at Maddie, offering a roughly textured but welcoming hand. Slowly He pulled her to her feet. She confessed that she was the one who'd touched Him. And, as if by habit, she recounted her story to the crowd. A few onlookers contorted their faces in disgust. The Rabbi said, "Your faith is what has brought you healing."

The Teacher opened His arms and Maddie leaned in to hug Him as several onlookers gasped. In spite of the gasps and clucking disapproval, the hug was hearty and earth-shatteringly long. It was as if the embrace held the deepest, most hidden parts of herself. Maddie melted in the light and love of it. It was the first time, in twelve years, that Maddie embraced someone without fear of defiling them.

Breaking the embrace, the Rabbi said, "Peace to you. And freedom from all of your suffering."

Before she could thank Him, some men burst toward the rabbi. They addressed Jairus, the man in royal garb, "Your daughter is dead. Don't bother the teacher anymore."

Ignoring what they said, the Rabbi told Jairus, "Don't be afraid; just believe." Then, He began walking toward Jairus's house.

Maddie wanted to follow. She wanted to thank the Teacher, hug Him again, let Him know how her life would be forever changed. But, He didn't let anyone follow except four of His fisherman friends and the forlorn father. Maddie wanted to tell Jairus that everything would be all right. In her heart she was shouting, *The Teacher's right, don't be afraid; just believe. Just reach out to Him and He'll be reaching in.*

Eight days later Maddie held two caged doves. Her plan was to present a sacrifice twelve years in the making. On her way up the temple steps to the Tent of Meeting, she looked at the birds. As expected, their round, purplish-green eyes implored clemency for innocent lives.

Maddie set the cage down on the top step, sat beside them, and began to reminisce. The day she touched the tassel of the Rabbi in Galilee felt so close and new and fresh. Yet it simultaneously felt far-flung. In some ways she still couldn't believe the unlikely herald of her healing. She wondered what would've happened if she hadn't reached out to the Rabbi. *Life is a curious thing,* she said to the birds. They cooed and waddled about their puny prison.

Maddie wondered about the twelve-year-old who had died on the day she experienced healing. In that moment it dawned on Maddie that she'd been redeemed from *twelve* years of bleeding; and the girl had died in her *twelfth* year. Now that she'd experienced the gift and love of the Rabbi, Maddie knew *that* couldn't be a coincidence. Like a bolt of lightning it struck her, with inexorable assuredness, that the twelve-year-old girl was alive. She was probably running around the meadow, picking wildflowers, playing hide-and-seek with her dog. *Just like me, she was freed from death. And now we're both alive to the joy and wonder and wildness of it all.*

Without a moment of hesitation, Maddie opened the dove cage. She reached in and took a bird for each hand. She stood, inhaled deeply, and released one. It swooped downward at first. Then, catching a current of wind it soared straight up to the precipice of the Temple and beyond. "For the little girl," Maddie said. Using both hands and bending her knees for extra oomph, she tossed the second dove into the air. It rose and glided in a fabulous flap of wings and wind. *For me.*

Maddie ran the whole way home. Her husband was in the orchard. She lavished kisses all over his head, hair, neck, and shoulders. Then, she kissed his mouth. In all her life nothing ever tasted so sweet.

*A woman was there who had been subject to bleeding for twelve years, but no one could heal her. She came up behind him and touched the edge of his cloak, and immediately her bleeding stopped* (Luke 8:43–44).

AFTER THE STORY

One moon after her sojourn to Galilee, reliable news came that—as Maddie suspected—Jairus's daughter had, in fact, been raised from the dead. Her name was Hannah. She'd grow into a woman, marry and started a family.

Over the next decade plus one, Maddie's family also enlarged. Each year she gave birth to a son. All together there were eleven brown-skinned boys with nests of curly brown hair just like Jacob. The farmer laughed and bragged to the neighbors, "Just like arrows in the hands of a warrior are sons born to a man. And—in my old age—my quiver is full!"

On the twelfth year after Maddie's healing, she bore a daughter. The baby girl was named Hannah, after Jairus's daughter.

Though Maddie had struggled through chronic illness, depression, and unbearable loss for twelve years, she was renewed, embracing the wonder of a life resurrected. She left a legacy for all women who reach out toward Jesus' kind and cosmic help, hope, and healing.

> *Faith is for that which lies on the other side of reason.*
> *Faith is what makes life bearable, with all its tragedies*
> *and ambiguities and sudden, startling joys.*
> — Madeleine L'Engle

# PONDERINGS FOR THE HEART:
## Reflecting on God's Love

In humility, honesty, hopefulness, and humanity Maddie reached out for healing in an unlikely place. She admitted her need, ignored the conventions of her day, and aimed for a few bright-blue tassels. Whether we're dealing with cancer, depression, arthritis, or a broken marriage, friendship, extended family relationship, we can follow Maddie's lead in reaching for a life of hope and healing. Sometimes the healing will be a cure to our illness, a mend to the relationship. Other times the healing will take a different form: peace or the ability to let go, set an appropriate boundary, forgive, or accept.

1. What part of Maddie's story sparked you? Could you relate to her need for healing? If so, what needs restoration, renewal, revitalization in your life? A relationship, a health issue, a diminished dream, a career derailment? Brew a pot of coffee or herbal tea, or simply sit quietly for a while and meditate on this and divine love's power.

2. Write a journal description or draw a sketch of a hurting part of your life. Then, write a supplication for help and healing. Flesh out the details of — or sketch an image of — what a restored life looks like to you. If you're ready, consider sharing it with a trusted friend.

3. At one point in the story, Maddie is described as having a mustard seed-sized speck of hope and faith (compare Luke 17:6). Do you consider yourself faith-filled? Find an object in your home that represents the spiritual side of yourself. Is it an empty cup, a quilt, a small stone, a cross or other icon, a piece of jewelry, a painting, a book? In this season of life, why is *that* object a fitting example of your way of reaching for Jesus?

4. As Maddie prepares to go to see the rabbi, spring is precipitating. But, she feels stuck in winter. Spring could be described as a season of fresh starts; and winter, a time when all is quiet and still, asleep, even seemingly dead. When people think of autumn, color, possibility,

and contemplation ring true. Summer can connote fun, freedom, playfulness, restoration. If you were to describe the season of your heart, what would it be? Why? Share your answer with a friend. Then, turn the question on her.

5. How does Maddie help you discover the Christ's presence in your daily life? Do you feel cared for by Jesus? Do you believe the hope for your hurt exists? If *no*, why? If *yes*, how could you take a risk, reach for, and receive it?

6. If you feel exhausted, isolated, even depressed by a chronic condition, take comfort in these words, meditate on them: God's compassions never fail. They are new every morning (Lamentations 3:22–23).

7. Touch can be healing. Remember the most captivating hug you've ever received. Where were you? What did the embrace feel like? Who hugged you? And why? What about this sensate experience made it memorable, meaningful to you?

> *God is every moment totally aware of each one of us.*
> *Totally aware in intense concentration and love . . .*
> *no one passes through any area of life, happy or tragic,*
> *without the attention of God with her.*
> — Eugenia Price, former atheist,
> best-selling Christian writer,
> author of 39 books, deceased

# HEARTBEATS:
## *Acting on God's Love*

1. Rest. Set aside a project. Turn off the TV. Leave the dishes in the sink. Don't answer the phone. Ask for help with work, or your children, or other obligations. Just be still. This may sound passive and nonproductive. But, sometimes in the stillest, most quiet, restful places we receive direction, a starting block for healing journeys.

2. Experience unfamiliar vistas. Read a new book. Go somewhere you've never been. Talk to a stranger. Mingle with a group of people you never imagined could become friends. As you broaden your horizons, a path for your healing, spiritual sojourn may become visible.

3. Create something that symbolizes your hopes for the future and the acceptance of your today. This could be a painting, a poem, a journal entry, a meal, a knit-scarf or blanket, a collage of magazine clippings, a sculpted piece of clay, a sandcastle, a song. Share your creation with someone.

> *Jesus acted on the law of love, not legalism. As far as we know, he never did anything about getting himself ritually cleansed. Because love, not law, is the great cleanser. In obeying this higher law he shocked everybody, including his closest friends, in his extraordinary and unacceptable ways of acting out love. Of being Love.*
>
> — MADELEINE L'ENGLE

# CHAPTER 3

# Dorcas Dies Before She Dies

## THE FACTS

NAME: Dorcas (translated from Greek, means "gazelle")

DATE OF BIRTH: New Testament Times

DATE OF DEATH: First time, during New Testament times (Second time, unrecorded)

OTHERWISE KNOWN AS: Tabitha (her Aramaic name, also meaning "gazelle"), a disciple, a learner, a member of the church at Joppa, a benefactress

SUMMARY: Dorcas was a dressmaker and weaver and follower of Christ living in Joppa, a coastal town on the Mediterranean Sea, 35 miles northwest of Jerusalem. She was known for her acts of charity (namely making clothing for widows and the poor in her village). Late in her life, Dorcas became terminally ill and died. Some of Dorcas's friends sent for the unpredictable, untamed Apostle Peter. He traveled to Joppa and miraculously raised Dorcas from the dead in Jesus' name. The story is found in Acts 9:32–42.

TRIVIA: Dorcas is the only woman in the New Testament specifically called a disciple of Christ. She is also the only woman whose resurrection has been recorded in Scripture.

ᴏᴹ Notable: No one had been raised from the dead in the early church so far as the records of Acts declare, but the faith of the believers was so great they *expected* the Lord to use Peter to resurrect Dorcas.

— *The Bible Knowledge Commentary*

ᴏᴹ Quotable: *Peter . . . got down on his knees and prayed. Turning toward the dead woman, he said, "Tabitha, get up." She opened her eyes, and seeing Peter she sat up* (Acts 9:40).

---

A Maxim of the Story: *Dorcas dedicated her life to helping the needy. Dying to herself, she lived for others and thus gained a full life. As some Christian mystics would say, Dorcas died before she died. When she literally died and was raised from bodily death, Dorcas once again chose to surrender her life to serve others. We, too, can gain in life by dying to ourselves. The death to self is about looking beyond ego self to see true self (the you God made you to be). It is about seeing beyond oneself enough to see others. And ultimately it is about experiencing transcendent love: the divine love of God that's beyond ourselves.*

---

The Mediterranean was particularly blue and tumultuous that Sabbath. If the Pharisees had seen Dorcas at work, weaving on her porch, she would've been chastised, condemned. Dorcas didn't hide her labor of love, though. Out in the wide open, hugged by oceanic breeze, she sat and wove a cloth the color of sea. Arthritic hands, knobby and aching, knew the rhythm and pattern of weaving by heart. Over, under, tug, and tighten . . . over, under, tug, and tighten . . . over, under . . . her hands instinctively danced and wove. As she created, the old woman thought of the Teacher who'd freed her to weave on the Sabbath.

He was warm and honest, a Galilean, a friend of women (unlike most of the religious leaders she knew). Dorcas had heard stories of how He'd been reprimanded for picking grain on the Sabbath, healing a leper on the day of rest. She'd memorized His response to accusations that He'd broken one of God's Ten Commandments. "The Sabbath was made for us. We're not made for the Sabbath," He'd said matter-of-factly, as if it should've been obvious.

One of Dorcas's dear friends, Mary, told of a time when the Teacher was accused of working on the day of rest. In the middle of the accusation a crowd gathered. The Teacher shared a story with them about a sheep falling into a pit. After the story, He'd looked into the crowd with a signature look of love and profound discernment asking, "Is there anyone here that has one sheep, and if it falls into a pit on the Sabbath would not take hold of it and lift it out?" Silence came over them. Even the religious leaders were tongue-tied.

The Teacher picked a blade of grass. He used it to draw an imaginary circle around the bystanders. Then, with grace and tenacity, He asked, "How much more valuable are all of you than a sheep?" He dropped the blade. "In healing this man, I have done something good on the Sabbath. This, my friends, is lawful." Immediately after the exchange the Teacher went to a nearby beach with His most devoted students, really His closest friends: twelve, including stinky fishermen.

Dorcas watched waves on her own beach, about a furlong from her tiny house, barrel onto the sandy seaside. While she watched, her fingers intuitively wove, and she imagined the Teacher building a bonfire for His buddies. In her imagination she could see the flames reaching toward a gray sky, and she could smell the smoke. She could see the Teacher praying with His friends, challenging them, laughing, dispelling their illusions about God with captivating and puzzling stories.

The picture was clear in Dorcas's mind, and she superimposed herself into it. Though she rocked and wove on her own section of beach, in so many ways she felt as if she was one of the guys — the thirteenth disciple — getting a broadened image of God.

For a woman who'd played by the rules, done the "right thing" for her entire life, following this Teacher sometimes felt awkward, against her grain, unexpected. Getting to know His ways felt as surprising as walking along the beach at low tide, discovering starfish, sea anemone, and shells usually hidden beneath the waves. But, she intuitively knew a closer look at Jesus, this Teacher, was a closer look at God.

The old woman stretched and yawned. She pulled a long strand of azure yarn from her skein. She'd woven hundreds of pieces of fabric like this in her lifetime: fabric she'd sewn into cloaks, tunics, chitons, or shawls for widowed, abandoned, neglected, or abused woman in the village. This fabric was special, though, earmarked to become a cloak for a thirteen-year-old named Deborah. Its yarn had just come off the loom. She'd dyed it with the most expensive and rare of all blues. When it dried in the sun, Dorcas had had to stand guard over it, lest the rare fiber be stolen by a nesting animal or greedy thieves.

Weaving the rare and vibrantly colored yarn was the best part of the process. The extraordinary thread spun and swirled capably between Dorcas's fingers, as if it knew how to weave itself. The weaver chose ocean blue from her favored and most expensive dye lot when she'd heard it was also Deborah's favorite color. Prayers always came with her weaving. *Lord, restore the joy of Deborah. Return to her what has been taken away by an evil, impetuous, broken man. Grant her new mercies every morning and a peace that washes her heart and mind like a wave.*

Dorcas's hands were aching, but she continued weaving and praying. *Because of her torment, enlarge Deborah's vision of you, God. Give her new eyes to see and ears to hear . . .* After an hour or so, the old woman's words trailed off, and the weaving became the prayer.

The swatch of blue grew. The skein unwound on the floor yielding a sense of accomplishment, progress. Dorcas smiled at the measurable artistry and prepared for another section of weaving. She felt as if the cloth were breathing, growing, taking on a life of its own. When she looked at her holy handiwork, Dorcas could picture the long, generous cloak it was becoming. She imagined the way it would drape over Deborah's scant shoulders. She hoped it would give the girl a sense of warmth and love, a kind of healing protection.

Deborah's story was crisp in Dorcas's mind. Two weeks earlier the girl, still tender and bruised, sat beside Dorcas on her diminutive porch by the sea. With terror still lingering from the attack, her voice was a shaky wisp, "I was on my way to the well. The sky was cloudy . . . the wind blew hard and strong. It was my turn to gather water . . ."

Dorcas put down the ecru cloth she wove and curved her arm round the girl's shoulders, "You don't need to tell me the whole story, beloved. I received your name in confidence. Let us just sit together and watch the waves while I make your cloak."

Whenever tragedy struck in the village, women of Joppa went straight to Dorcas. She was a safe place, a helper, a wise counselor, a harbor. Everyone knew their secrets would be safe with her. Dorcas treated her societal standing with respect, never using knowledge like a voyeur or gossip or judge. Though her position could be draining — even overwhelming at times — Dorcas's desire was to offer help and hope to widowed, abused, and bereft women, not to feast on the morsels of their tragic stories.

Together, Dorcas and Deborah looked into the long line of horizon made by endless sea and the sky that poured into it. Dorcas began weaving again. Within minutes, the girl's head drooped. She began rubbing the palms of her hands together incessantly. Dorcas set down the handiwork, took one of Deborah's hands in hers, and said, "You don't have to justify your need for a new cloak by telling me your story, dear one."

The old woman used a bent index finger to gently lift the girl's chin. When she looked into Deborah's eyes she might as well have been looking into an empty cave. Pupils were fully dilated, lids wide, brows knitted. Dorcas knew that sometimes — immediately after a trauma — it was too soon to talk. Dorcas also knew, from experience, that the evil weight of hardship unspoken could eat at the girl's insides, leaving only crumbs of her spirit behind.

"All right, child," said the old woman, setting down the handwork. "I am listening." The words came out in a gentle, unassuming, and comfortable way.

Deborah leaned in toward the weaver; she looked young and small and full of trepidation like a baby bird. "He came out of nowhere. He just . . . appeared."

The girl started to cry a little. With shoulders shaking, she continued in starts and stops, "He was much bigger than I. No one else was on the path . . . that was rare . . . he threw my water jug onto the path. It shattered into thousands of shards." She wept, then began again, "He . . . dragged me to a . . . hedgerow of bushes, stuffed a rag in my mouth, bound my hands with rope, and . . ." Deborah wept again, shaking and folding into herself.

Dorcas enfolded the girl into her arms. She draped the unfinished ecru cloth over Deborah like a blanket. The girl wept and rested in the old woman's embrace for almost two hours as sea crashed on shore. When Deborah finally sat up, Dorcas stood, stretching arms and torso, which ached from holding the girl interminably long. Dorcas didn't mind the pain, though; she knew full well that this little death to her self, this little self-sacrifice, opened a greater opportunity for the girl to heal.

Deborah looked away from the sun into a cloudless spot of sky. "It was strange, Dorcas," the girl said, as if she were trying to concentrate. "The day before I was raped, I told my mother that if anything like this ever happened to me, God would rescue me. I knew He would. I would call on the powerful, protective name of Yahweh . . . my assailant would flee, and everything would be all right."

Deborah's tears had been used up or she would've cried more. She looked fiercely into Dorcas's sagacious eyes for solace. "I called. But, God did not rescue me."

Dorcas let the sad statement linger like pollen in spring air, like a continually rising path of smoke from fire. In the fullness of that sullen and spacious and somber moment, she offered a small, gentle, *knowing* smile at the girl. Her words came out slowly, without an ounce of triteness or parental authority, instead with a grace that can only be born of shared loss, "God did not rescue you, child. Nevertheless, everything will be all right." The words felt solid and trustworthy: product of years of Dorcas's daily and lifelong wrestlings with the paradoxes of the divine. Still uncertainty and fear lingered.

Deborah wanted more solid sentiments. She wanted to put them on like one of Dorcas's pieces of handmade clothing, to hold them close to her bruised skin, "How do you know?" asked the girl.

"It isn't a knowing, beloved," said the old woman knitting again. "It is more of a way of feeling . . . really *seeing* God with my spirit. From this day on, your view of God will change. Yahweh won't fit into any box you try to make, like the one I tried to jam God into for years." The ocean crashed as if it were cymbals accentuating a particularly grand symphonic climax. "From this day on," Dorcas continued, "you will begin to see who God *really* is. Today you know that God doesn't always rescue His girls in the middle of a fire." The words hurt. They calligraphically etched themselves into Deborah's heart the organic, forever way lines had grown around Dorcas's smiling eyes, and animated forehead.

Dorcas took a deep, slow, quiet breath through her nose and continued, "Tomorrow, if you're open to it, you may learn more of the strange, mysterious, scary, and surprising ways of God. You may find out that Yahweh loves you in ways you never might have expected, or hoped, or imagined. You may discover that God is One who cries with us, who does not desert or abandon us in our darkest times. Like this new Teacher, always with His friends, God is with us, and can be in us, present to our deepest questions and fears and wounds. With us in our times of horror and hurt and healing.

A gull swooped onto the porch, trying to nab the bright-blue yarn. Dorcas vehemently swooshed it away, waving arms, stomping feet. Back in her chair, the old woman let out a chortle sounding like it would fracture her ribcage. Deborah couldn't laugh. Since the attack she hadn't even cracked a smile. "And, sometimes, God gives us companions to be with us, to protect us on the healing journey."

The girl began studying Dorcas's soft, agile hands, their skin with loose, soft covering over large veins and knobby bones. One of the hands reached for Deborah's.

"There is one thing you must remember, beloved." The hand was warm and as soft as it looked, "God may allow a fire in your life, but beauty will always be born of the ashes."

For the first time since the attack, the corners of Deborah's mouth began to upturn in the slightest, tiniest movement toward hope.

A swelling wave crashed on the shore bringing Dorcas back — from her memory of the day spent with Deborah — to the present. In the moment, Dorcas noticed how interminably achy her hands were. They begged for a break, so she set the growing cloth down in her lap. Fabric spilt across arthritic knees and draped onto sandy floor. Deborah's cloth, large with patterned purpose, had become a prayer woven on the loom of the old woman's body.

Dorcas studied the blue flowing over the edges of her lap, remembering the day she last wore that distinct color. It was when she was thirteen, like Deborah. The blue belonged to the bluest tunic Dorcas's mother, also a weaver by trade, had ever woven: a gift for Dorcas's birthday. For an entire early teenaged summer, Dorcas wore that dress. In that blue dress, she skipped rocks. In that blue dress she formed raisin cakes for her friends. In that blue dress, she took long walks by the sea and daydreamed about the boy who lived next door. The dress made her feel alive and able, and as beautiful as a Morning Glory.

It was also in that dress Dorcas called to God for help. That night, she ran away from home. She would never forget the star-filled sky, as a thirteen-year-old, when she pulled the beloved blue dress into hundreds of ragged shreds, burned it in the kitchen fire, and buried its ashes in the backyard.

Her first night away, Dorcas was taken in by a kind older woman. That night Dorcas had a dream. In the dream, Dorcas saw two strong, old hands. They were weaving, knitting . . . repairing a cloth: a tapestry of bright blue.

Today, sitting in the long shadows of sinking sun, Dorcas replayed the dream. She studied the hands that she'd wondered about for decades. *Did they belong to Mother? To the woman who took her in? Or could they possibly belong to someone else?* Without realizing it Dorcas's hands were weaving Deborah's cloth again. Over, under, tug and tighten . . . over, under, tug and tighten . . . over, under . . . The hands were unstoppable, even in pain they were at work weaving a hopeful intercession, *May she grow in grace and wisdom and healing. May she grow in grace and wisdom and healing. May she grow . . .*

Three months after Dorcas finished sewing the seams of Deborah's cloak and presented it to the girl, the old woman became terminally ill. Pain in her joints became so excruciating she couldn't get out of bed in the small upstairs room of her home.

In an effort to revive Dorcas, friends placed tempting, vibrantly dyed fibers beside her on the bed. They realized that the old woman's pain was insurmountable when her hands would not be tempted to weave. Mary, Dorcas's best friend, brought a pot of broth. Deborah and her mother steamed local vegetables and neighbors brought fresh water. Dorcas could not eat or drink for three days. Her already diminutive frame became skeletal. Breathing became arduous. A relentlessly high fever sent Dorcas into a quasi coma for a week.

During these seven days, widowed and destitute women came in hordes to visit the dying weaver. Congregating round the old woman's sickbed, they held up artfully woven and designed afghans, sweaters, shawls, cloaks, chitons, and tunics that Dorcas had made for them during destitute seasons when they couldn't afford clothing. They wept and prayed, shared their stories, and thanked the woman who'd made pieces of woven wisdom and hope for them to wear.

In and out of lucidity, Dorcas watched her handiwork seemingly float about the room in hallucinations. For her, each textile was a story, the story of a woman she'd loved and nurtured from pain toward comfort . . . toward beauty born of pain. Subconsciously—in her spirit—she heard the stories again, offered prayers of healing, again.

On the eve of a vernal full moon, friends gathered round Dorcas's bed singing songs of praise to God, and asking for a miracle. The old weaver was too tired to sing or pray. She raised her hands every now and then, though, seemingly knitting the air. Just before midnight, her breathing became irregular. A few breaths came, rapid and shallow. Then, she unexpectedly slowed down, inhaling awkwardly and deeply, as if she couldn't get enough oxygen.

Mary looked at Deborah, "Death is near."

Deborah held Dorcas's hand. It was as cold as the sea. She adjusted the bedding and noticed that Dorcas's legs were molted with large purplish splotches. "Look," the girl whispered to Mary with alarm girding her voice.

"I know," said Mary, gently tucking in the sheet in a gracious attempt to restore Dorcas's dignity.

Women took turns thanking Dorcas for her woven gifts and words. One woman thanked the weaver for five multicolored tunics made for five children after their father died. Some thanked her for blankets that kept infants warm; others gave thanks for shawls that had comforted and adorned after abuse. Deborah leaned close to Dorcas. She whispered in her ear, "Thank you for bringing beauty from my ashes. Every time I wear blue I will think of you."

For a moment it looked as if Dorcas was smiling. Suddenly, she took a long, deep breath; then, she was stone still. Most of the women left the room weeping wildly. Deborah, Mary and a couple others stayed to begin burial preparations: washing the body with soft sponges, anointing with fragrant perfumes, pressing fresh flowers into the hair above Dorcas's temples, drawing a nearly sheer, multicolored textile sheet over her corpse, beginning the work of good-bye.

To this day, no one knows whose idea it was to call Peter—who had been unharnessable Peter — now with a reputation in Palestine as one who healed in Jesus' name. But, when word spread that the disciple was in neighboring Lydda, two men were sent at once to fetch him. Whispers flew low and fast like nesting birds. *Perhaps Peter could raise Dorcas from the dead. Doesn't his name mean "rock"? Yeah, but, I heard he's about as smart as a rock. . . .* Women clutching sweaters and afghans, tunics and dresses, prayed and murmured, "I heard Peter healed a paralytic in Lydda. . . . May God bring grace to Joppa."

Just after noon, Peter appeared. He seemed larger than life with tanned, muscular arms and labyrinthine curls covering head and forehead. His escorts appeared bedraggled and exhausted. Peter, living on the edge, looked earnest and muscle-twitchingly ready. When he entered the tiny upper room where Dorcas had been prepared for burial, he calmly addressed the mourners there.

"Weeping women," he called, waving cloaked arms with holy zealousness. "There is work to be done."

The women bowed at Peter's authority and scuffled out of the room, still wailing loud, inconsolable wails.

The disciple looking at the dead woman noticed a slight smile on her face, a relaxation in her hands, a serene sense of rest about her, reflecting what Dorcas was experiencing.

For the first time in almost fifty years the old woman was free. She was light and mobile. In some cosmic, glorious, otherworldly way the wisdom of her years had inhabited a pain-free body. Looking about her, she noticed a sandy field of green grass. Without worrying about chronic pain, she began to run. Throwing back her head, pumping her arms, she took off. The tickle of air and grass felt good on face and feet. Her breath was deep and satisfying. She felt as if she could run for miles and days.

Nearing a bluff, Dorcas stopped. Looking over the edge, she saw ten thousand or more light-speckled seas stretching out over an endless land. Breathing deeply, she offered a prayer, "The heavens declare the glory of God!" Over and over she breathed the prayer: *The heavens declare the glory of God . . . The heavens declare the glory of God . . . The heavens declare . . .* Walking along the bluff's edge toward a path leading down to the beach, Dorcas experienced — all at once — the best parts of being young and the best parts of being old. Mysteriously, the most excellent parts of her self were divinely rolled into her present state of being.

As Dorcas neared the path's end and began to taste sea salt on her lips, she noticed a huge house. Looking at the A-frame gave her an overwhelming feeling of familiarity, of home. On closer inspection, she noticed that the house *was* her house, an exact replica of the tiny house in Joppa, but somehow it had been magically augmented and in perfect repair. From the distance Dorcas could see someone sitting on the porch, rocking in a chair that faced the sea. An azure cloth floated about the rocker's bent knees.

"Is that *me* on the porch?" Dorcas asked aloud. "Am *I* there, or here?" She felt slightly confused, and pinched her own arm. "Ouch!" Pain. *It can't be me. I am over here on the beach.* She looked down at her re-created feet. They were clad in comfortable leather sandals and planted in sandy soil springing with intermittent strands of tall grass. *If I'm here . . . who is rocking and weaving that gorgeous cloth on my porch?*

A prompting that felt something like her normal response to a friend's open arms urged Dorcas to run toward the house. She bolted in the direction of the seaside abode. Salty air kissed her cheeks and mussed her hair. Glorious. As she ran, the figure on the porch slowly came into focus. Shadow obscured the figure's face; so it was hard to tell if the being was male or female.

Dorcas slowed from the run to a walk. The porch weaver hadn't noticed her yet. A cardinal lit on the porch's railing. Dorcas inhaled with surprise when the bird started singing the melody to the *Shema*, a Hebrew hymn she often hummed on her porch while weaving. *Shema Yisrael Adonai eloheinu Adonai ehad* (Hear O Israel, the Lord is our God, the Lord is One).

The porch weaver's hands shifted in rhythm to match that of the song. Dorcas, standing mere cubits from the house now, felt compelled to study the weaving hands. They were large, strong, and capable, covered with a road map of veins and moving with gentle determination. They looked overwhelmingly familiar.

*Where have I seen those hands before?* She searched the annals of her mind. It took a moment; but, like a shoot emerging from the soil in spring, the place she'd seen the hands become apparent. *My dream . . . my dream . . .* she almost spoke out loud. *The hands are from my childhood dream.*

"Yes they are, Dorcas," said a most kind and generative voice emerging from the porch. Dorcas was taken off guard that the weaver knew her thoughts, her name. The voice continued, "I'm weaving this for you." The porch weaver held up the fabric, which further obscured the figure's face. The creation blew dancingly in breeze. It was precisely the color of sea.

Dorcas felt a catch in her throat. "My dress! That's the exact color of my old dress . . . the one mother made for my thirteenth birthday!"

The hat nodded and the gracious voice beckoned, "Dorcas . . ."

Without hesitation, Dorcas stepped toward the porch. Just as she felt wood beneath her foot, and bent down to get a glimpse of the face beneath the hat, she heard another voice.

"Tabitha, arise!" It was a commanding voice nearly yelling her Aramaic name, "Tabitha," it came again. "Tabitha, arise!"

Her momentary glimpse of the radiant image of the porch weaver's face — the most beautiful face she'd ever seen — immediately faded. Tears filled Dorcas's eyes. Opening wet lids, she beheld a startling sight: exuberant Peter. Without realizing what she was doing, Dorcas sat up. She felt dazed, disoriented, oddly homesick.

Peter took the old woman by the hand and helped her to her feet. As Dorcas stood, pain shot from her hips through her legs and into her lower back. She felt inexorably reluctant to walk. Peter prodded, almost pushed her toward an open window in the upper room of the tiny house.

There on the beach beneath the window stood a group of women, Dorcas's friends, and other followers of the Teacher. Dorcas felt dizzy, exhausted. She wanted to go back to the place of the porch weaver, back to the place where her body was pain-free. She wanted to see that face again. She couldn't help but cry more. Because of the tears, her friends looked like smudgy blurs. Peter positioned newly raised-from-the-dead Dorcas in the middle of the window, directly in the crowd's view. Dorcas's tears came in feverish, uncontrollable gushings now.

Peter announced, "By the power of Jesus, the Christ, Tabitha of Joppa has been raised from the dead."

Dorcas was speechless, weak, and writhing with pain. She wanted to yell at Peter, *"My name is Dorcas! No one calls me by my Aramaic name (the name of my childhood) here in Joppa. My name is Dorcas!"* Instead, she stood — too weak for words — at the window weeping. The crowd, assuming the tears were joyous, erupted with applause and victory shouts. Men waved fists in the air and whooped. Women embraced. Kids jumped up and down.

A trio, including Mary and Deborah, rushed to the front door of the house. Dorcas could hear their giddy voices as they clamored up her steps: "She's alive! Can you believe it? I thought she was gone for good! But, she's back . . . thanks be to God! Our friend has been raised from the dead!" Laughter followed, and pounding feet. Breathless, high-spirited by adrenaline and good news, the friends cautiously hugged a fragile and reluctant Dorcas.

Leaning with all her slight weight on Mary's shoulder, the old woman whispered, "I just want to go home."

"You are home, Dorcas," Mary tried to convince her friend with joy and breath in her voice.

"No. I am not," the old woman said acerbically. Then, gingerly, she walked to her bed, sat down, and with a quiet resolve asked, "Does anyone know where all my yarn is?" The yarn had helped Dorcas die before she died, in a sense. And, now, having died in body, only to live again, she knew the textile would be of enormous help.

Deborah ran toward a tangle of threads nesting in the corner of the room. She picked it up and brought it to Dorcas.

Gently pulling at the mess, Dorcas liberated a red thread. She began working it: over, under, tug and tighten . . . over, under, tug and tighten . . . over, under . . . Her hands instinctively danced and wove. As she worked she cried and said, "I guess there is still more weaving for me to do."

AFTER THE STORY

Dorcas lived for seven more years weaving and doing the work of helping to heal wounded hearts and bring hope in Joppa (while trying to release her bitterness at Peter for bringing her back. During her bonus years, Dorcas wove tunics for the wives of kings and paupers, scarves and blankets for the children of prostitutes and royalty. Though she daily yearned to return to the place where she'd run without pain, to look beneath the shadow to see the Porch Weaver, to sit on the eternal porch, Dorcas surrendered to her lot in life. While yielding to her daily reality, she relished telling the story of her life-after-death experience. Drawing out every detail of the glorifying sights, sounds, and the freeing feeling of it all: painting a verbal picture of her life-after-death reality for others to see.

Several weeks after her resurrection, Dorcas sat on her porch weaving a crimson prayer shawl for a recently widowed friend. Her hands and hips ached. She considered the miraculous events, pulling them through her mind like yarn through her fingers. Word had it that because of Dorcas's miraculous resurrection, there was an evangelism explosion going on in Joppa. Apparently hundreds, even thousands, were discovering and believing in Jesus as the Christ because of her story.

For a moment Dorcas stopped weaving. She looked down at knobby hands that had already lived through a lifetime of sacrifice. Her eyes felt heavy with the weight of tears. She blinked letting saline waters find etched paths down wrinkly cheeks. *What's a few more years in the name of Divine Love?* she asked the sea. It replied with an enormous crash of wave wetting and darkening the shore.

Though Dorcas struggled with chronic pain, and the fatigue that women who are caregivers often experience when they give too much, she left a legacy in her handmade clothes and acts of service to her community. Seven years after her resurrection, the old woman finally died and was able to return to a perfect kind of freedom and rest. When she saw the Porch Weaver again, she realized she was looking into the face of God. The Weaver smiled radiantly at the old woman, and handed her a skein of blue yarn. Beside God Almighty, Dorcas took a seat and began the work of weaving again.

Today, in honor and in the name of this biblical heroine, a Dorcas Society has been established. The society consists of groups of local people with the common desire and mission to provide clothing for the poor. Dorcas Societies are usually church-based, with the original society being founded in Douglas, Isle of Man (located in the Irish Sea), December 1, 1834. The catalyst for this group was gratefulness for being spared from an outbreak of cholera. During the outbreak, impoverished families in Douglas had to burn clothes and bedding to prevent the disease from spreading. Giving clothes to those in need brought the loss full circle into an act of service.

> In Joppa there was a disciple named Tabitha (in Greek her name is Dorcas); she was always doing good and helping the poor (ACTS 9:36 NIV).

> Religion that God our Father accepts as pure and faultless is this: to look after orphans and widows in their distress and to keep oneself from being polluted by the world (JAMES 1:27 NIV).

Dorcas died before she died — died to herself — providing unstinting care for others in her community. Because of her willingness to die before she died, Dorcas was acquainted with grief. Even in her sacrificial lifestyle, Dorcas found true life through glimpses of God working in and through her.

Ironically, in Dorcas's physical death, she found ultimate freedom, relief of physical pain, and connection with Divine Love. As we love others the way Dorcas did — as we die to self — we partner in God's lifegiving, enlarging love, and participate, bit by bit, in experiencing that kind of freedom.

> *Tears shed for self are tears of weakness, but tears shed for others are a sign of strength.*
> — BILLY GRAHAM

1. Christians speak of a love that comes in sacrifice. Sometimes this sacrificial description of love can — wrongly — keep women in sexually, physically, or emotionally abusive relationships. This is not the sacrificial love that Jesus embodied or Dorcas espoused. Theirs is a love that dies to ego self — or a narcissistic preoccupation with self — and lives to love others and God in ways that are life-giving. What are your preconceptions about, or experiences with, dying to self or sacrificial love? Share your thoughts with a friend or group.

2. There is a modern ministry of knitting prayer shawls. Many are given with a note or poem like this one:

> *A Yarn Intercession*
> *The yarn feels good between my fingers*
> *It spins and swirls capably*
> *As if it were weaving itself*
> *Instead of being crafted*

*I like seeing the skein unwind*
*On the hardwood floor*
*Preparing for*
*Another row of stitches*

*The creation: a shawl*
*Grows like a sunflower in my yard*
*With nurture and joy aiming for sun*
*Measurably and artfully stretching*

*My needles click a song of*
*Hopeful intercession*
*May she grow in Grace*
*And Wisdom and Amusement*

*Rows link increasing in*
*Patterned purpose*
*A prayer woven on the*
*Loom of me*
— SALLY MILLER

In honor of Dorcas, write your own hand-woven poem for a friend. Consider sharing it with her as an offering of Divine Love.

3. Maybe there is a Dorcas society near you. Check out Dorcas Society online or at your library or local bookstore. If Dorcas's story inspires you, consider serving with this organization. Bring a friend, or two . . . or more!

4. In the story, God used Peter to raise Dorcas from death and a dream. How did you feel about this well-intended ministry as you read the story? Did it bring up any personal memories for you? Have you ever felt like Dorcas when a well-meaning person tried to reverse something (an idea or experience or obligation) or dramatic life change occurred for you? Take time to think or journal about this.

What were your feelings around this event? Anger? Sadness? Disappointment?

Was a personal boundary violated?

How did you react/respond?

Is there something you would do differently if you found yourself in a similar again?

# HEARTBEATS:
## Acting on God's Love

1. Is there a women's shelter or PADS ministry near your home? Honoring the life of Dorcas, is there a way you could serve there in some way? Pay attention to a service opportunity that sounds exciting to you, that ignites your passion . . . follow that bliss, and give comfort or wisdom or beauty, or gift in ways similar to Dorcas (be sure to make it your very own way of serving).

2. Consider knitting a prayer shawl for a friend or neighbor or family member who is going through chemo, or another treatment for illness, or for someone who might be suffering from a broken dream or relationship or heart. There are free patterns available at lionbrand .com/patterns/81041AD.html.

3. In the story, Dorcas gave the grace of presence, understanding, and tactile goods (her woven gifts) to wounded women in need as a response to her own personal experiences with pain and woundedness. How have you — or could you — do this with your own life? In contemplating that question, consider using 2 Corinthians 1:3–5 as inspiration:

> Praise be to the God and Father of our Lord Jesus Christ, the Father of compassion and the God of all comfort, who comforts us in all our troubles, so that we can comfort those in any trouble with the comfort we ourselves have received from God. For just as the sufferings of Christ flow over into our lives, so also through Christ our comfort overflows (2 CORINTHIANS 1:3–5 NIV).

If you are sparked by this contemplation, devise a creative way to act on your inspiration.

# CHAPTER 4

# *The Woman of Endor Reaches for Life*

## THE FACTS

NAME: The Witch of Endor; we'll call her the Woman of Endor, Endora

DATE OF BIRTH: Before the Old Testament reign of King Saul (1020–1000 BC)

DATE OF DEATH: Sometime during the reign of King David (993–960 BC)

OTHERWISE KNOWN AS: Witch of Endor, the Medium at Endor

SUMMARY: Endora lived during war-torn times in Israel where she practiced the ancient ritual practice known as *necromancy* (consulting the dead in order to determine the future). In her day Israel's first king, Saul, banned all sorcerers from the land. Somehow, she survived the purge and remained in Israel—practicing her craft in secrecy—long enough to have a divinely appointed encounter with King Saul. During that encounter, Endora called up the spirit of the deceased prophet Samuel who foretold Saul's impending death. In an act of life-changing mercy, Endora killed her fatted calf and baked unleavened bread to share at the table with Saul on the eve of his demise.

TRIVIA: Endora's ancient Babylonian and Assyrian counterparts used several methods in their practice. Babylonians believed that *hepatoscopy*, divination by examining the liver of a sacrificial animal, allowed practitioners to "see into the future." Others used *augury*, searching signs in nature like the flight of birds, to foretell the future. *Hydromancy*, divination via mixing liquids; *casting lots*; *astrology*; and *necromancy* were also popular forms used by Endora's contemporaries.

 

ᴺᴼᵀᴬᴮᴸᴱ: [The] woman of Endor looked into the eyes of the most powerful man in Israel and saw terror there. Did the vision shake her? Did she recognize herself in him? Did her encounter with a prophet cause her to forsake her trade as a medium? — Ann Spangler and Jean E. Syswerda

 

QUOTABLE: "Look, your maidservant has obeyed you. I took my life in my hands and did what you told me to do. Now please listen to your servant and let me give you some food so you may eat and have the strength to go on your way." — Endora to King Saul (from 1 Samuel 28:21–22)

---

A MAXIM OF THE STORY: *For many years, Endora funneled her deeply creative and intuitive spirit into necromancy. At her unexpected and extraordinary encounter with Saul and his God, Endora's life turned upside down. On our individual spiritual journey, how do we respond to people, events, and circumstances along the way that may challenge our ways, perceptions, and belief systems?*

---

Endora had been on edge, restless, paranoid—scared about her future—ever since King Saul expelled the mediums and spiritists from her land. Her sleep was light and intermittent, overwrought with sweats in a tangle of bedding. Her desire for food had dwindled. Before the decree Endora lived to eat, enjoying aroma, texture, and taste of artisanal Israeli cuisine: flatbreads, dried fruits, spice-and-garlic-infused leg of lamb. The hostess within her soul reveled in feasting, gathering, moonlit dancing with family and friends. Now, she merely ate to live. Even raisin bread with honey, a favorite, couldn't wake up her sluggish, cranky appetite.

Immediately after Saul's banishing decree, Grandmother; Mother; and Endora's four best friends, Ruth, Tabitha, Essie, and Sarai, fled. Left behind were their oodles of jars filled with doves' livers, pigeons, rodents, and other mammals floating in vinegar-based, acidulated liquid preservative. Along with those: feathers and bones, a box of mismatched dice, a few precious handwritten and artfully illustrated astrological maps. The plunder was an inadequate, empty reminder of their once ebullient, laughing lives. Endora, alone in the house, rummaged through abandoned pickings feeling a lot like the misfit menagerie. Her only accompaniment: the flickering warmth of fire flames.

Exodus from the town of Endor had quickly occurred, sullen with fear and in the middle of the night. Endora wanted to flee with the other women. But, she didn't want to leave her house—the house Father finished building mere months before his death by stoning. A neighbor had turned Father in to the authorities for practicing augury, foretelling the future by observing the flight patterns of birds and other natural occurrences. His death had left a gaping absence in Endora's life. It made the house that much more precious and symbolic to her.

To Endora her father's house was a refuge. Its walls held precious memories. Memories packed with the colors, sounds, and aromas of her childhood: Mother's engaging laugh, the songs Father played every night after dinner on his slightly out-of-tune homemade stringed instrument, the hundreds of healing homeopathic treatments created and administered there, the soft purple blanket she was wrapped in on the day she was born. The memories were warm and good, like the scent of flatbreads, which used to be baked daily over kitchen fire and broken open at supper. By staying at the house, practicing her craft — necromancy — in shameful secrecy, and waiting, Endora hoped to maintain her rights until the day her elderly mother and best friends could return to Endor. But fear for her safety, anxiety about the future, were her only constant and unwelcomed companions.

Several months after the mass departure, Endora laid her achy body down on warm, sandy ground near the front entrance. It was one of those disarming summer nights when the chill of evening never sets in — even after the sun has disappeared behind the horizon like an actor backstage.

Endora had had seven customers that week. Four different sets of parents wanted to contact sons who'd perished in wars with the Philistines and more. Two widows needed to say a last good-bye to deceased husbands. And there was the sister of a boy who'd been eaten by a wild beast, looking for assurance that her sibling was living safely and happily in the afterlife.

Rubbing red eyes as she gazed into sparkling, luminescent night, Endora thought, *If I have to try to call up one more dead person, I may go to the grave myself.* The work was difficult, exhausting. It called for a kind of spiritual and emotional energy that, when expended, left her feeling beyond empty — alone. The darkness of dealing with the dead got to her. Even though Endora's goal was to find a glimmer of hope for those still living, delving into the dark chasm between life and death for so many years had been taking a toll on the medium.

Every muscle in her body melted, completely yielded into the warm ground. For the first time in weeks, it seemed as if sleep would be able to find her. Endora's bed beckoned. In a friendly voice it seemed to say, *Come, find rest. I'm waiting for you.* She tried to get up. Her body resisted any kind of movement, though, the same way a boulder seems to stick to ground.

During this rare solace, this unavoidable moment of stillness, Endora noticed a dazzle of shooting stars showing off in the blackened sky. For the first time in weeks, the future did not occupy her thoughts. Enrapt and enchanted, she watched, wondering what Father might have said about the stellar signaling. *Maybe I should start studying astrology. A change in the direction of my craft might not be the worst idea. I'm ready for something new, something invigorating, beyond my limits.* Fears for herself, fears about her future safety preoccupied her. She felt tempted to channel the dead for some answer — for solace — but had no energy for that intense work.

After at least an hour of awe at the shining spectacles, the medium felt herself nodding, then dozing on and off. her body resisting sleep. Not wanting to spend the night on sand with scorpions and other pests, Endora willed her hurting body to rise. Standing, she caught a jolting sight. A band of what looked like three men approaching from the dark distance. *I don't have the strength to do another consultation tonight,* she thought at first. Then, with a small gust of summer breeze, a chill of sobering fear came over her. *Maybe I've been found out. Perhaps these men are coming to me — in the night the way they came for Father — to take me to the Place of Humiliation and . . . stoning.*

As quick and lithe as a scared cat, Endora slid into the house and began hiding evidence. In one movement she obscured boxes of dice and astrology charts beneath the bed, stashed fermenting livers beneath a lean-to bench, then covered it in black muslin. She tore the star necklace from her throat and threw it under the rug. Her heart raced. The blood running through her veins seemed to bubble at rapid boil. Her breath was irregular; cheeks flushed crimson when the three strangers appeared, as if by instantaneous materialization, at her front entrance.

Endora turned toward them, breathing heavily, smoothing her robe, tightening the rope belt about her waist. The tallest one caught her eye. His body was cloaked. His face concealed by a large hood. Only a scant amount of his face and anxious searching eyes could be seen in the shadow of the hood. He stood between a short, portly guy and another, thin and skeletal. In a low yet commanding whisper, he asked, "Will you consult a spirit for me?"

Endora studied the men. They were definitely not from Endor. There was something refined about their countenances and manners.

Yet, their clothing was tattered, drab, unornamented. Reticence came over the medium as she considered the ragamuffin crew. They'd probably be unable to afford her behemoth fee to contact the dead in order to see the future. *How can I rid myself of them?* she wondered. Suddenly, she got an intuitive whiff of something strange, something ominous and foreboding. *Is this a trap?* the witch wondered, looking with squinted and transfixed eyes at the strangers.

With each passing second the tall one seemed to get more frantic, his pupils dilating because of the dark and his unmistakable, near hysteric fear. His voice was a short, clipped whisper that was simultaneously hurried and commandeering. "I need to get a word from someone who has passed . . . someone I will name if you let us into your house." It was as if the man — besot by his own desperation — was oblivious to Endora's fear and the way she examined him in vexed scrutiny.

Standing with shoulders squared in the frame of her front entrance, Endora continued sizing up the strangers. In a moment of brilliance and bravery, she decided to test the trueness of the tenacious trio's request, "Do you not know what King Saul has done?"

The men stood silently at the threshold, feigning unawareness. The thin one kicked at sandy dirt. The tall one pulled a handful of golden coins from his clothing and began shuffling them between large, brown hands. The coins clinked enticingly.

Endora, trying to block out the coins' alluring song, continued, "Saul has expelled the mediums and spiritists from his land." She waited for a telltale flinch, shifty eyes, or involuntary eyebrow raise. None occurred. Still the medium stood her ground, placing clenched fists on hips, unconvinced of the authenticity of the request. Another shooting star descended into the dark. With its soaring descent, an image of Endora's father blasted into her brain. In a flash she saw his lifeless bloody body splayed in disrespect and disregard on the ground. His face and limbs dotted with purplish-blue bruises.

The only Levitical law Mother had taught Endora — as a warning against getting caught — echoed along with a ghastly laughter in her mind: *A man or woman who is a medium or spiritist among you must be put to death. You are to stone them; their blood will be on their own heads.* The flight-or-fight reflex surged through Endora's cells. It was too late to escape.

She felt trapped. She'd have to find a way to outsmart the strange visitors, perhaps with a litany of questions, a parlay of words — or she'd have to bluntly ask what she feared most.

Her words surprised Endora as they flew out of her mouth like angry bees from a disturbed hive. "Are you here to set a trap for me and bring me to the Place of Stoning?"

The tall man who made the request, with earnestness in his voice and steady eyes, swore, "In the name of my God, and as surely as He lives, you will not be punished if you do what I ask."

Endora's body twitched with defensiveness, taught muscles, a tightened jaw ready to fire another dozen questions. She was ready to flee or build a fortress of deception. But, with the tall one's words and a slight touch, something inside her soul yielded. The true north of the witch's intuition told her that the stranger was being completely honest. He would be safe. Almost instinctively, Endora took three steps backward into the house making room for the mysterious visitors to enter. With a welcoming sweep of her arm, she said, "Please, come in."

The men bent over to remove dusty sandals. With a gentle, reverent eagerness accompanied by discomfort due to the unique circumstances, they entered and sat in a row on an opulent, well-padded couch. The place smelled of earth and freshly burnt incense. Endora took her typical spot on the rug in the center of the floor. She could feel the star medallion digging into her left leg as she positioned herself directly in front of the visitors. Reaching her hand beneath the rug, she retrieved the trinket and hung it back around her neck, arranged her legs in a pretzel, and squared her shoulders. Out of habit Endora used the back of her hands to brush errant strands of shiny black hair off her high forehead. And, in a sweeping motion, she flicked long locks over her shoulders. Settled into her space, the medium was wide awake and ready to commune with the dead.

Her eyes, gorgeous, almost black, and enigmatic, looked at the tall one. With a gracious earnestness in her voice, she asked, "Whom shall I bring up for you?"

"Bring up Samuel," the man's voice shook as if he knew what the reading would foretell.

Endora nodded, closed her eyes, let her head fall back so that the ends of her hair tickled the ground. It seemed obvious to the men that the medium had entered a kind of altered state. The tall one hid his head in large hands, not daring to look. The robust one and the skeletal one leaned forward on the edges of their perches to better observe. They watched as the woman's upper body peacefully waved like the leaves of a palm tree in the wind. She was mesmerizing and beautiful to behold. The corners of her mouth curled into a smile. She looked strangely serene as if her mind glided on some kind of still-watered supernatural pond.

Without warning, the witch sat erect, opening her eyes wide and looking directly at the tall one. Her jaw dropped open, creating a gaping cave of a mouth out of which exploded a bloodcurdling scream at seeing Samuel actually appear. The scream morphed into an accusation, "Why have you deceived me? You are Saul!" She stood up and, with herculean strength and anger, lunged toward King Saul, the tall one. If his large and lean bodyguards hadn't grabbed the woman's arms she would've tried to strangle the king.

Still kicking and pulling to get at Saul, yet restrained by his men, Endora half-listened while his majesty tried to placate her, "Don't be afraid." His words were commanding yet careful. "I am not here to bring you harm. Truly, I need your help." Slowly, he got up from the couch and walked toward Endora and gently touched her arm. His words and touch, for a second time, disarmed. She stopped struggling to be free of the men and listened.

"Call Samuel, I beg you," said King Saul, "and tell me what you see. I am going to war and he may have a word from him." His voice was steady, eyes warm. The king gestured for both of his men to release Endora. As they did, she felt as if a pigeon of trust had roosted on her shoulders. Slowly, deliberately, the medium sat back in her spot on the rug. The men again sat in a row on the couch, transfixed. Endora adjusted her star necklace. She adjusted her hair, closed her eyes, and returned to a place of still readiness. Slightly swaying, her knowing smile returned.

"What do you see?" demanded the king in an over-eager whisper.

Endora's voice was placid, almost melodic, "I see a god coming up out of the ground. A *god* . . . not an *apparition* like I normally see. He's surrounded by light . . . white, pure, warm rays of . . . light . . . and life and . . . beauty." The medium inhaled deeply as if she were taking in a sweet aroma from the vision. "I hear songbirds and . . . trickling water in the distance." The opulent sight was nothing like Endora's typical nefarious, dark, deathly, stench-filled manifestations. In this moment, the room, her father's house, was becoming the sanctuary Endora had always imagined it to be.

Encouraged by the woman's words, King Saul asked, "What does the spirit look like?"

Whispering, afraid the loudness of her voice would dematerialize the glorious sighting, she replied, "He's wearing a long, lush robe . . . the color . . . of new wine. His hair is long and white like the breast of a dove. His eyes shine are. . . holy . . . solemn. It is as if he is here to tell . . . *me* . . . to tell *me* . . . something."

Saul knew at once that the man Endora had summoned was the Ephraimite judge and prophet, Samuel, who'd appointed (and later rejected) him as Israel's king. Immediately King Saul prostrated himself, burying his face into the rug. *Let him bear good news for my family and me,* he hoped, prayed.

The spirit of Samuel was so strong in the room now that it was as if the prophet stood in the flesh before the curious quartet. With a powerful timbre, Samuel's voice blasted into the room. He addressed the prone king, "Why have you disturbed me by bringing me up, Saul?"

Saul lifted his head and looked in the direction of the voice, "I am in trouble. The Philistines are waging war against me." The king's voice shook, the words scraping dry tongue and throat, "God has turned his back on me. He doesn't answer my prayers and refuses to speak to me through dreams or my prophets. So I am here, consulting a medium, hoping to hear your advice."

Samuel's voice boomed with tornadic anger now, "Why do you come to me now when the Lord has done everything I predicted? You did not obey. And because of that, He has torn your kingdom from your hands and given it to David." The room was sick with quiet. In another booming, bursting backlash, Samuel continued, "Now, God will hand all of Israel, you, and your sons to the Philistines . . ." Saul once again buried his head.

Endora continued to gently sway. She could sense the anger, still found herself lost in the glory of the sighting, a serene smile remaining on her countenance. Saul, divergently, looked up, his face heavy and ashen. Blood rushed from his extremities and began swirling within his empty bowels. He sat up leaning in disbelief against the couch. The prophetic voice blared one last mantic message, "Tomorrow you and your sons will be with me."

The oracle-bearing Samuel vanished. The medium slightly shivered. Despite his ominous news, Endora longed to hear more from the prophet, to gaze again on his beauty, ask what his words were for *her*. Instead, noticing Saul overtaken with fear and falling on the ground, she ran to help. Kneeling beside the forlorn king, she longed to comfort him.

Endora wiped her sweaty brow with a generous flap of her gauzy sleeve. "You appear to be very weak." The king moaned and drew his knees to his chest in a fetal pose. His men rushed to help him. Though Endora was not a mother, a maternal urge the size of a mountain overtook her, and she, too, urged, "Have you had anything to eat today?"

Saul, shaking in a way that inhibited lucidity, could not respond. His henchmen vigorously shook their heads. The portly one whispered, "His lordship has not eaten all day . . . or night."

It was now well past midnight. Endora's exhaustion had been replaced by adrenaline. With one hand, she squeezed Saul's shoulder. With the other she smoothed back his hair. He began to relax. His shaking ceased. Looking intensely into the king's eyes, the medium spoke with authority that surprised her, "Look, I — your maidservant — have obeyed you. By doing your consultation, I took my life in my hands. Now, please listen to me." Saul gave out another groan and rolled back into the fetal position. Endora stroked his back compassionately, "Let me give you some food so you can have strength for your journey."

With the meager amount of strength remaining in the king's body, he refused the meal, "I will not eat!" he groaned.

The king's men rallied with Endora. "We cannot possibly make a journey to the battlefield with no food in our stomachs. . . . The night has closed in on us. We'll be *eaten* if we do not eat. . . . Let us take this woman up on her kind offer. It is our only assurance of help and hospitality." The men hooked arms with their king. Slowly, he got up from the ground to sit on the couch. Once seated, he nodded at Endora. With this unspoken acceptance of her offer, Endora was set into frenetic motion. Grabbing a large, recently sharpened knife, she disappeared into the night.

The jugular on Endora's only fattened calf was easy to find. In one quick motion her main artery was slit, and the calf lay still on the ground, spilling blood that made a warm, salty deathbed. Artfully and with respect, Endora butchered the animal the way her father had taught her. While she worked, she couldn't help but consider the ways her daily dance had been interrupted by Saul, his men, and the bright-beautiful prophet.

It was mind-rattling that the God of Israel had brought a spirit . . . a *spirit*, not an apparition. She longed to tell her mother and her friends about it. If she got the chance, she'd explain that the spirit of Samuel was divine (nothing like the grim, gruesome apparitions she typically channeled). She'd tell them that, in one moment, her way of seeing the world had shifted, her paradigm had changed. She didn't know exactly how, or what would happen next. But, she knew she'd been changed by this unexpected encounter. It seemed to have opened her to something new and different. Something—Someone—alive, truthful, omnipotent, and unconcealed. A life-bearer, a whisperer of light and love and star-like brightness.

Under the evening sky now laden with grey clouds, Endora imagined the women telling her she was crazy. Maybe. Or maybe she was about to change her ways forever. Clouds seemed to float dangerously close to earth. Endora inhaled, trying to focus her attention on meal preparation. With fresh air flooding her brain, the medium felt tempted to consult the prophet Samuel. She wondered what his word would be for *her*. Then, she wondered if he'd already spoken a word to her, an unspoken word that would remain with her long after this night.

The dead calf moved with a postmortem nerve twitch, startling Endora and reminding her of the urgent nature of the moment. Knowing she had much to do to prepare the king's last supper, the meal on the eve of his death, Endora lit the outdoor spit. Flames grew, gobbling tinder and igniting logs. The woman arranged calf ribs and legs for perfect roasting, then ran back to the house to prepare bread dough for the meal. For she knew in her heart that the prophet's words would be fulfilled.

The men monitored her actions in a tired daze as Endora skillfully mixed seeds and pulverized grains with water until the concoction formed a sticky, yeast-free dough. As she kneaded, the woman was conscious of and sensitive to the brooding moment. Yet she was acutely aware of her limited time with the guests, and she yearned to ask them about Samuel and the God she glimpsed — through him — for a mere moment.

"I am sorry about your reading, Saul," she said with mind racing, hands kneading.

The king stared at the ground. "God's will be done," he said in a flat voice that dropped off with weakness and exhaustion.

Endora patted the dough and tucked its ends toward the middle, forming a rounded dome. "Do you not find comfort that you will be with the prophet soon?" she asked.

The king, still looking down, didn't respond. She tried again, "It seemed to me that the place to which you are going is glorious, full of peace and beauty."

The king remained silent.

Endora yearned to ask more questions. But, she knew that if the bread didn't get on the fire soon, the meal wouldn't be ready before daybreak. With three doughy loaves in a huge basket, the medium headed back to the fire. One of the king's guards, the portly one, followed her.

"Thank you for your kindness to the king during his final hours," he said, warming his hands near the roaring, nearly blue flames.

"I would rather serve him a meal than wrestle with his men," she said with a grin.

The guard burst into laughter, "You don't have to worry about wrestling with me again. I know, without help, I probably wouldn't be able to take you anyway."

Now she was laughing. Turning over the loaves with a long, flat paddle and staring into the flames she said, "May I ask you some questions?"

"About what?" asked the guard looking graciously and with curiosity at Endora.

"About your God." said the witch.

"Ask anything you wish." He plopped to the ground, ready and nonchalant.

Dozens of questions flew around Endora's mind like bats on a summer night. The bread and meat, baking too quickly, added to her maddening furry. She blurted the first, probably most important inquiry fluttering in the forefront of her brain, "Why does the God of Abraham, Isaac, and Jacob prohibit witchcraft?"

The guard picked a long dry blade from a tuft of grass to stick between his teeth. He was cautious and kind with his words. "Our God wants people to trust Him . . . I think it is written that He created every animal of the forest and that He knows every bird."

As he spoke, Endora mentally drifted off. She began thinking about Father again. She could see him, clear as day, studying the birds, charting their migratory patterns, discerning the meaning of their movements. *If God owned all the animals, knew all of the birds*, she thought. *Then, surely He could predict the future more accurately than any man . . . or woman . . . who watched those very birds.*

The portly one was still talking "According to the Scriptures, God promises to provide for, protect, and love us. All He asks is that we honor and respect Him explicitly . . . that we let our faith come from and rest in His graces alone."

"Sounds easy," said Endora removing the perfectly baked bread from the outdoor oven and placing crusty loaves in her basket.

"In thinking, it is easy. But, living it can be more challenging than you could ever imagine . . . especially when life gets tough and it feels like it might be a good idea to take control of our lives into our own hands."

Endora wanted to continue the conversation. But, the bread was a perfect golden brown and warm; the meat was charred on the outside, rare with juice on the inside. It was time to sit up and enjoy the meal before it got cold.

Inside the house the men pulled stools up to Endora's long wooden table. The thin one poured wine, the portly one heaped medium-rare pieces of veal on everyone's plates. Endora picked up the three beautiful loaves, perfect. She passed them for the guests to admire; then broke a piece of bread for herself.

Bowing his head, the portly guard gave thanks for the meal. "God, we are grateful for this food. We thank You for Endora. We thank you for Your words. We trust You, even with the prophecy that You brought us from Samuel."

For a moment it was quiet. Only the crackling of the fire outside and a few crickets could be heard. The king began to sob. The prayer continued, "With the grace ascribed to you, comfort my friend, Saul, as he and his sons battle and then depart to be with You and Your prophet. We will praise You forever for what You have done. In Your name we will hope for Your name is good. Amen."

After the meal, the medium watched the men walk to the boundary line of her property. As they disappeared into the twilight she could taste the salt from her tears on her upper lip. Going against her typical inclinations, she didn't try to stop the sadness. It felt warm and wet and seemed to wash her heart. In this rare moment, she welcomed the open, tender way it made her feel.

Though tired, Endora considered the immediate gratification of Samuel coming up. She felt tempted to trust in his powerful words alone. There were so many things she wanted to ask: *How does one hear the voice of God the way you do? How can I get close to this way of living? Is it possible for a life of necromancy to be transformed? What will happen in my future? Can a woman like me live with trust in God instead of grasping at the future through struggling to commune with the dead?*

Something in Endora's spirit (the portly one's words still echoing within, perhaps) told her that a reading with dead objects through putrid fumes wouldn't bring the answers she needed most. She walked over to the fire. Flames grew and danced, offering twisting tendrils of smoke to the heavens. Endora felt like the fire: breathing, growing, wanting to offer herself in a new way to a reality bigger and beyond herself. She longed to stay by the fire and dance out the feelings the way she and mother and the other witches had: sky clad. Instead, she pulled the star from her neck, gave it a good-bye kiss, and gently tossed it into the flames. As it fell, it reminded Endora of the shooting stars she'd been watching all of her life.

## AFTER THE STORY

Two days after the departure of King Saul and his men, word came to Endora that Samuel's prophecy had come true: the king and his sons were dead. It is believed that this made Endora inexorably sad and yet somehow fortified her. Sitting on her rug, did she try to picture the king with Samuel? Did an image of him in the place of beauty and light she'd seen in her vision give her a modicum of peace?

Two years to the date after the death of King Saul, during a time when Endora had become known in the nation of Israel, Mother and Endora's four witchy friends returned to Endor. Endora told them about her encounter with the king and his God. For the next three decades, some believe that they approached ways of trusting, hoping, walking with the God of Abraham, Isaac, and Jacob.

On a particularly star-filled evening during the third summer after the women's return, it's believed that a rather portly guest showed up at their front entrance, hoping to enjoy another meal of veal and flatbread. Endora obliged. After the meal, the portly man ended up staying in Endor, marrying Endora, and becoming the father of her seven little girls.

Endora and her mother, friends, and daughters never forsook their wisdom, and deeply intuitive natures and skills.

## PONDERINGS FOR THE HEART:
### *Reflecting on God's Love*

*The woman had a fattened calf at the house, which she butch-
ered at once.*

  *She took some flour, kneaded it and baked bread without
yeast. Then she set it before Saul and his men, and they ate.*

(1 SAMUEL 28:24–25)

Endora for many years funneled her deeply creative and intuitive spirit
into necromancy: the only way she thought to help others (and herself),
to live, to connect with spiritual realities. We're all on journeys of faith.
On these journeys, at times we might be close-minded, self-absorbed,
or set in deadly ways. Or we can walk with eyes wide open, seeing
spiritual surprises, and respond to them with grace, empathy, kindness,
and openness.

  Endora's heart allowed her to give the gift of help and hospitality
to King Saul on the night of his death. Her service, coupled with an
open mind, allowed her to enter into a new spiritual space. In the same
way, when the strings of our hearts get tugged toward compassion,
do we listen? Respond? Obey? And when the journey of compassion
introduces us to new ways of growing in faith, do we respond in open-
minded willingness to enlarge, see, grow?

1. Endora experienced the vision of a prophet that shook her to the core.
   The prophet shared the voice of God, truth. Instead of false answers
   from trying to consult the dead, Endora was witness to Samuel's trust
   in the living God of Abraham, Isaac, and Jacob. Have you had any
   paradigm-shifting visions and encounters with art, books, or friends
   that have enlarged the way you picture God and pursue a life of faith?

2. Endora lived with a constant fear of the future. It drove her into dark,
   deadly spaces. Her encounter with the God of Abraham opened her
   to a different future. She may have forsaken her trade as a medium

(which was illegal during her time), to instead use her gifts of wisdom and intuition, and become something and someone new. Has anything like this happened for you? Have you had any experiences parallel to Endora's where you've been called from destructive practices into life-espousing, centering, peace-giving new ways?

3. For years Endora tried to find assurance and love and comfort in one way: through the practice of necromancy. Like her, it is sometimes easy to get caught up in common practices of our day that espouse false hope, even trying to work our way to heaven, following the letter of the law instead of the spirit of the law. How can we, like Endora, put down practices that make our wheels spin, and instead receive the gift of faith and trust?

4. Jesus called the Last Supper and shared between Himself and His closest friends. Jesus broke bread for His friends. We remember this every time we take Communion. Is there a way you are being asked to break bread for a neighbor, friend, work associate, or child? In an act of compassion and kindness and hospitality, consider who God might be calling you to invite into your life, to commune with. You might choose to write a list of names that come to mind.

# HEARTBEATS:
## Acting on God's Love

1. King Saul lived in a power-over paradigm. He ruled. He set rules. Though he yearned for a deep connection with his God, he lived by the sword and died by the sword. Endora was threatened, yet she opened her home. She shared bread with even her enemies. Endora and King Saul entered into a dialogue that changed both of them. What can we learn about God's love as we notice these themes in Endora's story?

   Consider someone you know — someone of a different faith tradition, perhaps a neighbor or a business colleague. Consider inviting them over for coffee. Open your heart and home to the possibilities of sharing God's love on a deeper level because of this connection. Consider your openness or resistance to this invitation.

2. In this creative story about Endora, she had a star necklace that symbolized her practices. As she encountered an enlargement in her life, she removed that old symbol. Is there a symbol you wear around your neck to represent your thinking and practices? A heart? A dove? A cross? Or, perhaps, a different symbol? Take a moment and, using the format below, write a poem about your symbol:

   Today I wear a _____

   It means _____ to me.

   Tomorrow I will wear a _____

   because I see _____

   and feel _____

   with _____ circling myself,

   resting by my heart.

3. If marriage changed Endora, it would have become a part of her journey to trust God. How have central relationships in your life changed your spiritual journey? Collect some flat rocks. On each, write the name of someone who has had an impact on your faith journey, who has been a stepping stone on your path of deepening faith. Place the stones on a windowsill, on your desk, or somewhere you will regularly see them. Thank God for the people who have come into your life, who have helped you experience God's love more deeply.

# CHAPTER 5

# Song Listens to the Melody of God

## THE FACTS

NAME: Song (based loosely on the life of Xiao Min)

DATE OF BIRTH: Sometime during the 1970s in Hunan, China (As a child of Chinese farmers, with little education, Song's actual birth date may not be known.)

DATE OF DEATH: Song is alive and well.

OTHERWISE KNOWN AS: The Writer of China's New Song Hymns

SUMMARY: Song is a peasant girl from a small village in China's Hunan Province. Her life as the daughter of farming folk is all at once extremely ordinary and unexpectedly extraordinary. Due to the One Child Policy, and as is the custom for families in China with more than one girl, her parents planned on placing Song for adoption when she was ten days old. The day she was to be taken away a flood ravaged Hunan.

Song remained with her family, was raised on the farm, and attended a local school. During junior high Song suffered from a debilitating sinus infection which led to talks with her faith-filled aunt about God; and ultimately—despite the chagrin of her parents—to a visit to a Christian church. At the end of 1990, with her life deeply rooted in the church, Song composed her first hymn. Today, Song has written more than 900 Chinese Christian hymns.

TRIVIA: Though Song is unable to read notated music, she is a prolific composer. Once her refrains received some notice, Song was given a little tape recorder. She records her hymns on the recorder, writes down the lyrics and a friend creates the notated sheet music, or manuscript.

NOTABLE: Song's hymns have been transcribed and recorded in a 930-song collection, known worldwide as the Canaan Hymns. Song's music is sung throughout China in the Three Self Churches (state-sanctioned Protestant Church) and Home-church assemblies (state-approved meetings of some 15 persons inside homes). They're also sung in Chinese churches around the globe. They've become the sacred Christian songs of the Chinese nation, the heart-cry of 70 million Chinese Christians.

QUOTABLE: "I know God has put a love for my country in my heart. Psalm 33 says: *Blessed is the nation whose God is the Lord.* When I read this, I thought of my own country." — Xiao Min
"It had to be that God inspired her [Xiao Min]. I don't care how talented she is; maybe she could have come up with nine or ten hymns on her own. Never so many! It is our wonderful God."

— XIAO MIN'S FATHER

A MAXIM OF THE STORY: *Song lives an everyday life in her particularly personal eastern surroundings. As she feeds chickens, takes walks on China's grassy green sod, goes to church, hangs out with friends, sweeps her kitchen, raises her kids, she is open to hearing the voice—really the* melody—*of God. As she opens her soul, her self, her moments and days to the divine, new songs are born in her. The music is a gift to Song. She graciously shares her gifts with friends. Passed aurally from one person—one province—to the next, the songs have ultimately become a gift to China and the whole world, really. As we open our hearts to the melody of God, and share God songs with others, we can partake in Song's creative work.*

The Chinese night was dark and ominous. Like a stomping-mad giant, the Songshan mountain range forced bulging blackish-gray clouds and thunder into the small valley villages of China's Hunan province. Ma Ma sat beside a window in her humble, dirt-floored farmhouse. Air heavy with moisture and the sweet fresh smell of rain flooded through cracks around the casement. Nine-day-old baby Song slept — oblivious to the foreboding forecast. In her dream the babe drew imaginary milk with tiny rosebud lips.

As Ma Ma watched her daughter she thought, *It looks as if my girl is kissing an angel.* Her hand cupped the infant's downy head; her forearm cradled the small warm body. "*Wo ai ni,*" she whispered *I love you* into the sleeping baby's curly ear. The utterance and her arms wrapped around Song tighter than usual. It was as if holding the baby close would prevent the inevitable: dawn when the Strangers would come to take Song away.

Wet tornadic wind whistled though cracks in the farmhouse. A shiver went up Ma Ma's spine. Ma Ma didn't know who the Strangers were. She didn't want to know. Arrangements had been made. There was nothing she could do to stop the dominoes of her life from clicking to their ultimate evasive end. Ma Ma was stuck in a corner created by China's One Child Policy and her familial status. She already had two children. One boy. One girl. Because of her farming station in life, the government permitted two children. But *three*? And *another* girl? This one would have to be quietly released, or . . . *placed* away.

Song began to fuss. Ma Ma held the babe on her shoulder; patting her back, blowing the sound of the far away sea into her ear, "Sh. Sh." The baby settled. Ma Ma remembered. She remembered her third pregnancy and the way women of the village shot her the evil eye as her belly become large and luminous like the moon. She remembered feeling as if China bent toward her like an old woman whispering a curse in her ear, *A second girl is a sign of weakness; this is a bad omen for your family.*

Ma Ma drew Song close to her heart hoping for comfort; but only felt the disparaging heaviness of love and hope deferred.

Dawn came. But, the sun did not wake. It was hidden under impenetrably black clouds raging rain on Song's little village. Ma Ma still slept in the chair by the window with the babe in her arms when Ba Ba startled them awake, "A flood. There's been a horrendous flood . . . No one can get into the village . . . no one can get out!"

"A flood?" asked Ma Ma. Her heart expanding . . . floating with the hopeful news.

Ba Ba raced about the room, a chicken with his head cut off. "We must buoy the hen house with extra protection . . . check the feed . . . I'll go see if Ye Ye and Nai Nai need anything."

In the middle of Ba Ba's stormy, circuitous whirling Ma Ma was stilled, centered: as calm as a portly smiling Buddha staged at a family altar. A personal flood of relief washed over her. Song would not be taken today (or *ever*, Ma Ma decided in a moment of epiphany). The baby was warm and wondrous in her lap as Ba Ba continued buzzing about the room.

"Come and sit for a moment that we might talk," Ma Ma beckoned her protective and urgent husband with a calm clement timbre in her voice. Ba Ba, hands on hips, eyebrows knit into an angry squiggle, stomped toward his girls. Sitting on the edge of a rustic chair beside his wife, he said, "There's too much to be done to sit for *tan hua* talk."

Ma Ma was calm and resolute, "There's nothing more important than what I'm about to say right now. I think this flood is a sign from heaven that Song is to stay with us." Father settled deeply into the chair. His forehead relaxed, brows sinking restfully closer to his eyes. With head bent toward the east he slightly kowtowed toward Ma Ma. Nothing more needed to be said. Nothing was. He completely agreed.

The baby stirred emancipating chubby baby arms and tiny balled up fists from their swaddling blanket. She was too little to socially smile. But, when she opened her almond eyes, they looked as bright and smiling as a grin ever could be. It seemed as if the wise, bright-eyed little one understood the divine news: a gift of forever home, *jia*, had come on the clouds.

Song knew in the deepest home of her heart that there was no place she'd rather grow up than China. Her country felt like a companion, a friend, *Péng You,* to her. When she walked beside grassy streams or fed Ba Ba's chickens on the dusty red soil of the farm she felt a love — an ardor — that was deeper and fonder, redder than Chinese-red nationalism.

*Wasn't it true that if you dug deep enough into earth you'd always find red, iron-rich soil?* she considered.

Every Chinese farmer's daughter knew that. Iron-red was the vein running through all of nature, holding it together, giving it life. When Song walked through the fields yellow with flower or gazed at China's grassy green hills crowned in clouds; she sensed this red ever Presence. To Song the Presence was creator, holder and maker of life. The wise women in the village called the Presence, *Heaven.* That seemed too impersonal of a name to Song. Besides, it wasn't mysterious and distinctive, special, and distinguishing enough. *There must be another name for the One who made all I see and love,* she thought.

Song's aunt, Ayi, called the presence, *Jesus.* During walks and dinners and visits over tea, Ayi told Song she thought the Presence was actually the God of Abraham, Isaac, and Jacob. The God who whispered in the wind, painted sky with sunset, parted the Red Sea. The One who wanted to redeem people so much He became a baby, to live and die in the world He made for them.

"Ayi," said Song in an epiphany during one of these talks, "Often I've studied the sky, the birds, the flowers, trees, grass, and the hillsides. I always knew they were the work of a Creator. Now, because of you, I know that Creator's name."

Ayi smiled a soft, demure, knowing smile. She put a welcoming arm around her niece.

"I feel as if I've been friends with Someone for my entire lifetime and finally . . ." Song said, leaning her head into a niche in Ayi's shoulder, "Finally, I've discovered His name. My heart feels like a kite soaring above Mount Songshan. Over and over it keeps saying, 'Oh, that's His name . . . that's His name: Jesus!'"

The virus attacked when Song was a preteen. It wasn't that bad in the morning so she'd rise and ready herself for school. Song enjoyed each morning's lessons. But, by lunchtime tsunami-sized waves of nausea came over her. Dizziness made her feel as if the slightest touch or even an unfriendly glance could topple her. Under the strain of the sickness she felt like a rigid noodle, undone, made limp and malleable by a pot of rapidly boiling water. Many days she felt too sick and weary to complete the school day.

On one of these days when the illness felt particularly nefarious, Song was curled on her bed in the early afternoon hoping sleep would anesthetize her pain. Auntie noticed the girl's suffering and sat beside Song on the bed's edge, stroking her long lacquer-black hair, "Why don't you come with me to church tonight? We'll ask God to help you get over this sickness."

Song barely lifted her head, "You know how Ma Ma and Ba Ba feel about church. I don't want to get them mad."

Ayi leaned closer to her niece. Song could smell the savory broth they'd had for lunch on Ayi's warm breath, "They'll never have to know where you're going. Just tell them you're visiting me; that I'm teaching you to knit."

That evening, before Ayi could finish her dinner, Song was urgently knocking at her aunt's door. "Are you ready to *knit*, Ayi?" asked Song with a spark of surreptitiousness glinting in her almond eyes.

There was no instantaneous, miraculous, angel-trumpeted healing for Song at church. Still, something in the service slowly, artfully, began to pierce her: a red thread stitching together quilt blocks of her scattered spirit. She wondered if it was the synergy of people gathering, singing, clapping, just *being* together in the presence of God. It was good to be in the sanctuary, others surrounding her, feeling part of something bigger than herself. *You are not alone in your pain*, the moment whispered . . . Jesus seemed to say.

Music danced on the sanctuary's floor in percussive bass notes and cascading melodies. It floated in swirls of vocals and contemporary-hymnal piano up to the church's balcony. Sweet sonorities encircled Song, enfolded her. The music was part of the quilt forming within her, wrapping Song from the inside. Melody and lyric beseeched the sick girl to breathe deeply, close her eyes, take in sound and scent and Spirit. *The God I've met in Ba Ba's fields is here . . . in the music . . . in this place,* she wanted to shout. The melody of God she knew from nature met her here in this unlikely place, in this church with this new Chinese Christian community, in these songs.

Song looked down on the congregation, at hundreds of glossy black-haired heads. Strangers and some friends she recognized from school clapped and swayed. They smiled and raised golden-hued hands. Ayi smiled too. She reached over and held Song's hand. Together they sang lyrics lauding love and redemption, lauding Jesus who died by crucifixion yet lived to see heaven in resurrected forever love. The song was good. But, something was starting to feel strange, unfamiliar, even foreign to Song. During her flash of feeling, she couldn't identify exactly what evoked the alien notions. Writing them off as product of her newness to the congregation and a naturally shy spirit, she sang out loud and strong and long.

A handful of church meetings later, Song began to feel a difference in her body. The excruciating sinus and head pain remitted. The dizziness and nausea — gone. She could breathe and exert energy for a full day's worth of schooling and farm chores.

Luxuriating in the freedom of good health, Song sat beneath a solitary bent tree in her father's field. She bent her body gently kowtowing and praying, "Lord, I've felt You changing my life. I believe in You. I believe you've healed me. Thank you!" In that moment, though Song could not feel or see it, a heavenly creative gift took wing and nested in her like one of Ba's chickens.

At the end of 1990 as Song prayed, read the Bible, walked to church, fed Ba Ba's chickens, and daydreamed, something strange and wondrous started to happen. Without warning, she'd find herself humming new melodies, contemplating lyrics, forming choruses and verses. The music came in blasts and spurts, sometimes even waking her in the night, demanding her attention; a nurturing voice. In a breathy alto, new songs emerged in lovely perfect pitch. Song labored with most of her tunes for five to ten short minutes; inevitably she'd find herself proudly and unexpectedly holding a newborn hymn: modern, made in China, fresh from God.

Song couldn't share the tunes with Ma Ma or Ba Ba. The couple was still ambivalent about her church attendance. Song still had to sneak out to go to the meetings. *Ayi might like the homemade hymns*, Song considered. But, her fear of criticism, comparison with *real* hymns from the West — the hymns they used in church, translated from *Meigua* (American; the beautiful country) — caused her to keep the music to herself.

For a while the girl guarded her tunes as if they were hungry, homely orphans found in the market or alongside a road busy with bikes, overstuffed pickups, and pedestrians. It was peculiarly splendorous holding the unexpected, wiggly, life-laden gifts; being the only one to know about their existence. Still, the hidden infant hymns couldn't take their seclusion for long. Daily they begged and cried, wailing to be shared.

In the village on a lonely Sunday afternoon as a big red ball of sun began to set, Song sat on a rustic bench beside her young friend, Péng You. Spontaneously and softly, she started singing one of her hymns. The melody was simple, yet compelling. The words spoke of thanking Someone who had chosen her in the midst of the crowd, who had found and loved her. Péng You lost in the romance of it all said, "Song, that's a beautiful melody. Will you teach it to me?"

Looking to the right, then to the left to be sure no one else was listening, Song began to sing. One phrase at a time, she invited Péng You to echo her melody. Three times through the hymn Péng You had the tune and words set to memory. The melody was liberated. So was Song. In the ecstasy and fun of the moment the girls didn't notice the earth completely swallow the crimson orb of sun. The eastern air began to chill, "We'd better get home before it gets even darker," Song said standing to leave.

Péng You, still singing the song, also stood and began walking away from Song. Five steps into her departure, she hesitated and over her shoulder, hollered, "Where did you learn this, Song?"

Nervous and giddy, Song called back into the cold air, "God taught it to me."

That night Péng You taught Song's hymn to her family. In her bed, on the other side of the village at around midnight, Song sang the melody too. Her mother heard the song and sat up in her bed to listen. A slant of moonbeam spilled into the room from Ma Ma's window. *Who is that singing?* she wondered. *That sweet, perfectly pitched voice can't possibly belong to our daughter!"*

She shook her husband's shoulder, rousing him from a deep sleep. "Ba Ba," she whispered. "Listen!"

Two parents, awake in the deepest darkest part of night, listened to a pentatonic masterpiece as it glided through humid air to their expectant ears. Eyes wide open, they sat in their bed awestruck, alert, ardently admiring the daughter they would've lost if the flood hadn't come.

In church the next autumn, Péng You and Song sat next each other. The melody they shared at dusk on the village bench rang around the sanctuary. Guitar, piano, strings, and percussion provided a rich, full accompaniment to voices reaching for the rafters. During a swollen upbeat in the introduction of the tune, a congregant sitting in front of Pungyo leaned to her friend and asked, "Who wrote this beautiful hymn?"

Péng You scooted to the edge of her seat and whispered into the woman's ear, "Song wrote this hymn."

The woman turned around and stared directly at Song, "How could *you* write this? You never go anywhere and I don't think I've ever heard you speak a word. You're usually hiding in the corner during church meetings."

With reserve, humility, and a dose of good humor Song cracked a smile, and with head bowed started singing along to her own God-given melody.

The next three hymns were Song's too. One of them efficaciously declared God's love for China. *Zhong guo ren (Chinese people) are God's children, finding peace, finding home / If God had one breath left, He would give it for the Zhong guo ren.* Song's voice vibrated like timpani in her chest. She raised her head high, and for the first time, felt like family in her own church. As she sang, Song wondered what generated these feelings of belonging. *Could it be the moment in time? Her friend? The music? The music! It was the music — God's melodies — reaching into her chest, wrapping pentatonic fingers around her heart.*

In a moment of grace, Song realized that all the worship songs she'd ever sung — before God gave her the gift of music — were from America or Europe. Music from *Meigua* was good and meaningful and true. But, it seemed to lose something quintessential in translation: its context and essence, its life. It wasn't written for *her* or for *China*. It was distinctly western, foreign, other.

Song's hymn reached a crescendo. The voices of Chinese men and women, boys and girls, reached for a high note. As the note reverberated around the room, every head lifted high. Every eye sparkled with the wonder of being known and well-loved. Pentatonic fingers gripped their hearts too. This song — about God loving China, choosing China — became vividly incarnate because it was written for them, written by a girl who was one of them, written by a girl born of China. Church music from far-off lands existed apart from Chinese Christians like a planet on a parallel orbit. These hymns came near, orbiting hearts and home and lives well-known.

When the final cadence of the hymn was held in a frame of silence, Scripture was read aloud. Swept up in the power and poignancy of the moment no one remembers the exact text. Some speculate it was Mary's Magnificat:

> *I'm bursting with God-news;*
> *I'm dancing the song of my Savior God.*
> *God took one good look at me, and look what happened —*
> *I'm the most fortunate woman on earth!*
> *What God has done for me will never be forgotten,*
> *the God whose very name is whole, set apart from all others.*
> *His mercy flows in wave after wave*
> *on those who are in awe before him.*
>
> — Luke 1 (*The Message*)

Those gathered could see Mary in Song, a teenager, an everyday girl from a poor family, yet precious to God and bursting with God-news. In the moment Song didn't know if she'd ever compose another hymn. Still, in gratitude she whispered, *Thank You, God, for coming near to me and showing Yourself to China in a uniquely particular, eastern way.*

Song had never before seen the man who showed up smiley and tall on her father's farm just after breakfast. He greeted her parents in perfect Mandarin, then kowtowing to Song, handed her a small tape recorder. "I've heard your hymns, Song. Please record any more you create on this device; and if you want, I can take them to a music student at the Central Music Academy who will notate the songs for you."

During walks in the fields of her father's farm, at prayer meetings, on the narrow tree laden path leading to her church, in the deep of the night, at the dawn of day, Song recorded more than 930 hymns.

One autumn evening ominous with blackened storms, Song was on her way to a church meeting. The clouds reminded her of what she had been told about the night of deluge and flood in Hunan — the night she was to be adopted. Fear and disconcertion circled her heart like ravenous vultures. The experience, like so many others, inspired another hymn: *Lord, You have held my hand as I've ridden the storm. Please hold my hand again.*

The choir was massive and talented. The virtuosic instrumentalists were part of the renowned Chinese Ballet Orchestra. All were convened to record several of Song's compositions, which came to be known as China's New Song Hymns, and had spread across China like a scattering of seeds.

Song sat discreetly, in a sound booth, hidden beneath earphones that landed on the sides of her head like floppy pup ears. Strings and flutes majestically, even magically, played Song's simple, pure melodies. A soprano vocalist added her coloratura part, answered antiphonally by the tenor and baritone sections. The music swayed into a climax as brass, timpani, and the tutti choir joined. Cymbals crashed, timpani rolled, strings bowed into an accelerando. The main musical motif was recapped; and with listeners wanting more, the piece cascaded into silence.

Tears fell down Song's face at the end of the first take of the first score when all of the musicians began thunderously clapping. "What master wrote this piece?" asked the first violinist.

Xu Wenxing, a student from the Central Music Academy, stood and pointed at Xiao Min who hid in the recording booth. "She wrote this. Her name is Song."

The first violinist began to snicker. The rest of the string section and some of the brass joined him. "You must be joking!"

The conductor raised his baton, silencing the scoffers with a cut-off. Two sound technicians escorted a reluctant, almost embarrassed Xiao Min out of the booth and into the studio. The conductor, acknowledging the teenage girl, extended a hand toward Song and bowed. The musicians, in shock and awe, began vigorously, really thunderously, clapping again. As Song humbly bowed to her admirers and, in the deepest place of her heart, she kowtowed to God.

## AFTER THE STORY

Today, Xiao Min (our Song) has created more than 930 Canaan hymns (China's New Song Hymns). The songs have become the greater part of the Chinese Christian hymnody. They continue to spread across China and to Chinese congregations in the West via word of mouth and Chinese Christian websites.

On September 7, 1992, Chinese authorities arrested Xiao Min. She and several friends from her home church went to a jail in the Fangcheng area. While in jail, true to character, Xiao Min sang Canaan Hymn 51. It is a song about the way pine trees on the mountains face wind from every side. Yet, through the changing seasons they stand tall, reaching toward heaven, staying forever green. Ultimately released, the hymn writer returned home with a bruised nose and resilient spirit.

Today Xiao Min is married and the mother of two children. She lives in a village in northern China and continues to travel, teaching her latest hymns to congregations all over China. She can be found scratching Chinese characters on chalkboards and humming simple, life-changing melodies in Chinese home-church assemblies and Three

Self churches, in remote villages or bustling cities all over her homeland. (According to a source in China, Xiao Min probably moves around quite a bit, trying to keep a low profile and avoid alerting Chinese authorities.)

Through Xiao Min's creative work, Chinese-speaking Christian men, women, and children from Beijing to Birmingham have music that sings a new and unique heartsong. Because Xiao Min listened for God's voice and looked for His presence, she was given a new, healing, and pertinent song. She became His instrument to give songs of faith and inspiration to her people. Those of us who are listeners and see-ers may join in her journey.

> *He put a new song in my mouth, a hymn of praise to our God. Many will see and fear the Lord and put their trust in him.*
>
> (Psalm 40:3 niv)

> *"I think it would be difficult even for a doctorate student from Beijing University to write such lyrics. I know no student from my school, the Central Music Academy, who can write music like this."*
>
> — Su Wenxing

## PONDERINGS FOR THE HEART:
### *Reflecting on God's Love*

God's love comes to us through our unique and diverse geographic and cultural experiences. *The Spirit of God was at work within Song, drawing her to Christ before she ever knew a name for God.* Because of her connection with her Christian aunt, Song learned a name for God: *Jesus.* We all learn new names for God based on the Scriptures, and the spiritual guides and teachers we meet along life's journey. The relationships we have, mingling our life experiences, bring forth different metaphoric songs for different times in our lives. These metaphoric melodies become ways of experiencing God's love and expressing our love in return.

1. We encounter God's melodies — Godsongs — throughout our lives. If you were to describe the song God is singing to you these days, what descriptors would you use? Is the song lively, staccato, pianissimo, slow, drawn-out, dramatic, comforting? Is it a lullaby or a symphony or praise song, a jazz band combo, a march, or a ballad? Take a moment to describe the song you hear. Explain why you think this is God's particular melody for you right now.

2. Typically, Christians sing to God. A curious and unique verse in the Book of Zephaniah captures God singing to us. Consider studying this verse on the following page, and reflecting on its meaning using the meditative practice of *lectio divina*:

   Take a moment to meditate on this verse. Read the verse slowly aloud three times. The first time, listen for a phrase or word that stands out. The second time, reflect on what touches you (share that with a friend or write about it in your journal). Third, respond with a prayer or an act that you feel called to, based on the entire experience. Or more simply: listen, reflect, respond.

*For the Lord your God is living among you. He is a mighty savior. He will take delight in you with gladness. With his love, he will calm all your fears. He will rejoice over you with joyful songs.*

(Zephaniah 3:17 nlt)

3. What part of Song's story sparked you? Do you have a unique love-language or musical or worshipful way of connecting with God in Jesus? How would you describe this language?

*I think the Canaan Hymns are God's gifts to the Chinese people. When I sing hymns translated from other languages, I feel that I'm walking into the kingdom of God. Now it's like God walks into our hearts and takes care of all our needs through the Canaan Hymns. He encourages us when we are weak; He strengthens us when we lose hope; He gives us power when we need it; He guides us with these hymns. So I think the Canaan Hymns are absolutely right for the Chinese church. They touch me very deeply.*

— member of the Self-Church in China

# HEARTBEATS:
## *Acting on God's Love*

1. The psalmist expresses gripes and fears and worries to God, as well as abundant praises. Read a few of your favorite psalms. Perhaps read Psalm 37, 100, and 121. Take time to write your own song. If you'd like, create a melody to go with it.

2. Take a moment to think about what kind of music makes you feel close to God. Is it a symphony or a praise song or a rock ballad? Is it a folksy melody, an instrumental, or a capella piece? Take time this week to listen to that music. Tune in to your feelings as you listen.

3. Singing can be a uniquely resonant way of connecting one's body with God and with a community. We're not all made to be singers. But, we can definitely all make a joyful noise. Take some time to sing in worship with a gathered body of believers. And find time to sing to God on your own. It could be in the car, or, of course you could ubiquitously sing in the shower.

# CHAPTER 6

# Joan of Arc's Great Absurdity

## THE FACTS

NAME: Joan of Arc

DATE OF BIRTH: January 1412 (Domrémy, France)

DATE OF DEATH: May 30, 1431 (Rouen, France)

OTHERWISE KNOWN AS: The Christ of France

*❧* SUMMARY: Joan claimed she had visions of God asking her to recover her homeland from English domination. She led the army in an astounding string of victories; and was ultimately convicted of heresy by English regent John of Lancaster, and burned at the stake.

*❧* TRIVIA: In a dream, Joan's father saw her marching with an army. He told Joan's siblings that if the dream materialized they should drown her.

*❧* NOTABLE: If anything could have discouraged [Joan of Arc] the state of France in 1429 should have.

— KELLY DEVRIES

🙐 QUOTABLE: She said, "I fear nothing for God is with me."

---

A MAXIM OF THE STORY: *Joan listened to what she identified as heavenly voices and took them up on a great absurdity they proposed. We can dialogue with God through prayer and His Word, and embrace His supernatural power in our lives.*

---

In a simple, two-story, white house nesting on fifty acres of bucolic French soil, twelve-year-old Joan slept. Lightning bugs publicized summertime. Joan dreamed of hikes to the pond with her four siblings and lingering dinners by the fire. Her steepest worries were how to get blueberry stains from beneath her fingernails and whether or not she'd menstruate before autumn. Mom said a change in her female body would transform Joan into a woman. Joan longed for the metamorphosis. But, she wondered what it'd feel like physically — *and to become a woman. It must be strange, alien, yet — somehow — completely normal*, she imagined.

The air was damp and heavy in the Domrémy countryside. It oppressively clung to Joan's arms, legs, and neck. She wrestled around in bed trying to find a cool spot on the sheets. Mom cracked the door to Joan's bedroom; Joan closed her eyes, feigning sleep.

"*Bonne nuit*, my angel from heaven," Mom whispered, punctuating the blessing with a kiss on Joan's forehead. "Sleep tight. Tomorrow is a big day," she said smoothing Joan's hair. "We're going to Notre Dame de Bermont."

Joan's heart leapt like a spotted lamb. She stifled a smile until Mom's skirt was swishing toward the doorway. Joan willed herself not to stir until, through tiny slits in her eyes, she saw the last bit of Mom's shadow skim out of the room. Joan's heart quickened, anticipating the next day's sojourn. Days at church — singing, lighting candles for the Virgin, tasting bread and wine, watching sunlight dance on stained glass, smelling incense — rivaled summer nights digging for crawfish in the Meuse River.

Her friends thought Joan's religiosity, her obsession with the spiritual, weird. She didn't care. There was something about God that enticed her. Even greater than the sound of Siren voices that had intoxicated Odysseus.

On the way to Notre Dame, she'd pray, prepare her heart — for the teasing.

The boys of Domrémy seemed to ominously line the entire path to church. They'd recess their games of ball to laugh at her. "Joan's going to church *again* . . . what a surprise," Michel would start.

"Why don't you go straight to the convent, Joannie?" Simonin would ask.

Colin would answer, "She's on her way." The boys would kick dirt in Joan's direction, wiping their noses with bare hands. Some would coarsely gesture.

As she thought about the ridicule, Joan wanted to yell her favorite expletive into the dark of the night. The powerfully abusive word made its way toward her lips but she held it in the way she held in air during confession. Even from the bed, she felt the urge to claw the boys, punch their pugilistic noses. Her breath was heavy, her fists clenched. *Remember your oath, Joan.*

Part of the holy life, Joan thought, was making oaths to God: one not to swear, one to remain a virgin until marriage, one to honor and obey her parents. In this moment, she kept her promise. In the meadows of the Meuse River valley, it was more difficult. She often renegotiated and rationalized her divine deals, whittling them into figurines, little idols, which suited the moment. To Joan's way of thinking, the Cuss Promise never applied to cursing brothers under her breath or profaning farmhands (while kicking them in the shins) if they looked cross-eyed at her. And the Purity Promise could be bent just a bit on spring days when Simonin wanted to hold Joan's hand under the burgeoning, white-blossomed apple tree.

Despite what Mom called the "tempestuous temperament of a thoroughbred," Joan held on to the integrity of her promises (whittled down though they were). They lined her mind like statuettes on a shelf, renderings of the woman she hoped to become.

*When will I be a woman?* she wondered as a slant of moonlight illuminated the night and her sheets. A magnificent, translucent paper moon, hanging in the center of her window, caught Joan's eye. Enchanted by the lunar daze she began again to consider the gifts of growing up when suddenly, a voice startled her.

"Mom, is that you?" Joan was shaking.

A litany of "voices" seemed to descend into the room. They were a mélange to her, a combination of the voice one sometimes hears in the back of one's head, and voices that communicate more subtly through nature, art, and music. *Clearly, this isn't Mom.* The day before, at noon, in her father's garden, Joan thought she had heard similarly strange voices. But, she'd ignored them like a consignment of pesky flies. Tonight there was no ignoring, no escaping.

Tonight the voices were stronger, more persistent, swooping down like the unavoidability of fruit bat wings that sometimes tangled in her hair on summer nights. The chorus of sounds, all at once, scared and intrigued Joan. When she gave in to fear, the sounds were indiscernible. When she calmed herself she thought she could hear something that sounded like whispers mingled with rain song.

Joan feverishly wanted to know what the voices were saying. But, the more worked up she got, the more they muddled, as if they might be speaking foreign languages. She tried to still herself a bit, letting her head be heavy on the pillow, relaxing her legs and the grips of her fists.

Suddenly, she thought she could discern a few words. When she was completely still, Joan sensed the voices calling like a friend with a secret, *Joan . . . Joan. Joan.*

She waited in the afterglow of the call, hoping for a ubiquitous follow-up. None came. "What?" she demanded in an impatient, curious, and slightly self-conscious whisper. Her eyes darted, hands beginning to sweat.

She took a deep breath; tried to still again. The response came immediately, clearly. It was steady and maternal in nature: *Don't be afraid, Joan.* A breeze lifted gauzy curtains. Joan caught her breath. She was awestruck when—for some indiscernible reason—the command completely centered her. Believing she was in the presence of something or *someone* holy, Joan got out of bed and knelt on the hard, oaken floor.

With head bowed, eyes peeking through her eyebrows toward heaven, she asked, "*Who* are you?"

*I'm St. Michael*, she sensed a soothing baritone, pleasing and pure and as satisfying to Joan as spring honey right from the comb.

*I'm St. Catherine. And I'm St. Margaret*, seemed to Joan to twitter and buzz, beelike bells to St. Michael's honey-gold-ostinato. The more Joan listened, the more she got used to the sound like wind rustling leaves. They sounded to her, all at once, precise and organic, airy and otherworldly, perfectly intoxicating. Listening to them was better than smelling fresh grass, burning embers, or lavender.

Joan was enjoying the midnight visitors. They made her feel chosen, grown-up, inimitable. She felt light enough to fly to the moon until they whispered, *We want you to drive out the English and bring the Dauphin to Reims for his coronation.*

This drove her prone to the floor. Though her body was prostrate, her eyebrows knit into a V, and her face pinched like a currant. After a minute of silence, she lifted her head, "Drive out the English?" She massaged her temples, "What are you talking about?"

*You'll know when you need to know*, she heard the trio serenely assure.

This was too much to ask of a girl. If God was going to give her a mission — an absurd one at that — she at least deserved to have all of the pertinent information up front and crystalline. Joan stood up, putting hands on her hips. She felt as if she were reprimanding the boys on the way to Notre Dame.

In a low, determined voice, Joan said, "You're all crazy . . . you have the wrong house . . . the wrong bed . . . The. Wrong. Girl!"

She heard the trio break into a gentle, rippling laughter that bounced off the ceiling and walls of her room, toying with her own playful spirit, her inner spark and spunk and sassiness — reasons Joan felt she was the perfect choice.

Somewhere deep within Joan knew. She wanted to go against the grain, be brave, belong to God. She couldn't help herself. Before she knew it, her arms flew from her hips to embrace her own sides. She was bent over, laughing. It was the kind of laughter that can make you wet your pants and feel dizzy when it is all over.

Hung over from the guffawing, she spoke even though she sensed the saints weren't listening, "I'm just a farm girl. I'm only twelve! I can't even read or fight (well, I guess I slugged Jacquemin pretty good the time he stole my last piece of apricot cake)."

*Be strong and do the work,* the phantasmal voices seemed to say. Then, like a ribbon of smoke trailing to heaven, they disappeared.

During Joan's teenaged years, other girls her age were dating and being dumped, flirting and courting, plotting chess-like maneuvers toward matrimony, throwing chastity belts to the wind. While they braided hair, batted eyelashes, and became bawdy with the boys; Joan was becoming brave.

From age twelve to sixteen, she entertained her ephemeral voices two or three times a week. Some days she'd wait around, sitting on the corner of her bed or under the blueberry bush in Dad's garden—wherever she'd last heard the voices—hoping, expecting, *needing* to hear them again. They'd become like best friends to her, exciting, softening, beckoning. With each encounter, Joan became more poised, persuaded. She was getting accustomed to the voices, starting to know and love them.

One autumn, Joan and her best friend, Isabellette, picked round red apples and ate them beneath the Lefèbvre cellar door. As she wiped sticky sweet juice from her chin, Joan told Isabellette, "When I hear the voices I feel such great joy that I wish I could always hear them."

"I wish I heard voices too. Sometimes I lie in bed hoping they'll visit me. They never come," said Isabellette. She twisted her hair and looked at the sky. Then, she looked at her friend. "What do the voices sound like, Joan?"

"They're hard to describe, Izzy. Try to imagine putting the sound of rain, your favorite song, the punch line of a good joke, and a fanfare in a bowl and mixing it up."

"You're the oddest girl, Joannie." Isabellette smiled, fluffing the hem of her skirt.

Joan leaned against the cellar door, putting her hands in her pockets. "Last time we talked they told me to write a letter—a letter to the king asking for permission to travel with the army."

Her eyes wide and round, Isabellette took a gargantuan bite of apple and started viciously chewing. Juice dribbled from both corners of her mouth.

"I dictated the letter to Jacquemin. And you'll never believe it . . . yesterday I got royal permission to battle against the English."

Isabellette stood up and began to pace the gravel ground. "A letter to the *king*? Permission to travel? You're crazier than I thought you were, Joanie."

"I know it sounds loony, Iz. Even *I* think I'm nuts. But, I feel as if I *have* to go."

Standing up and looking down at Joan, "No you don't. No one has to do anything but breathe, milk the goats, weed the gardens, eat, and sleep . . ."

Joan crossed arms over her flat chest. "If you heard the voices, you'd know what I mean. I *have* to go. I really do. Joan closed her eyes, "And, Izzy—" then she opened her eyes, "don't tell anyone. But, I'm scared."

"I'd be scared too." Isabellette said softly, kindly, sitting back down beside her friend at the cellar door.

"I'm going to miss the farm, and Mom's brioche. I'll miss summer at the river and church and my own bed. I might even miss Jacquemin." Joan hugged her knees and sighed. Then lowering her head, "I'm definitely going to miss you."

Isabellette realized Joan was serious about her barmy idea. "I'll miss you, too, Joan," she said. Both girls began to cry. Half-eaten apples lay on the ground beside them.

On a particularly cold and blustery day in February of 1429, the snow danced in miniature tornadoes. It spun across the meadow whose grassy green had yielded to autumnal gold and finally austere sparkling white. With the snow, a bass voice started visiting Joan every day. *It speaks the best French I've ever heard*, she thought. *Like only God would.*

Listening to the voice, this time, felt as substantive to Joan as taking the Eucharist. It surprised her that she didn't shirk, shrink back, or try to brush the voice away when it requested, *Recover your homeland from English domination.*

Joan had come to trust the loving, inspiring, convincing, *really* self-convinced timbre of the voice. Its confidence in her was a fortification. She wanted to listen, to hear, to act. She felt ready when the voice, with words more exhilarating than a first kiss, exhorted, *Daughter of God, go on, go on, go on! I will be your help. Go on! Go into France.*

Against all odds, Joan turned into a knight. She hacked off her hair, borrowed hand-me-down armor, horse, and—yes—a banner.

Mysteriously she began to possess a kind of confidence that surprised and buoyed her to what she felt was God's cause.

Mere days after Joan sensed the voice's urging, February 23, 1429, eve, with six men, and that flag held resolutely high, Joan road through the megalithic Gate of France, on her way to Chinon.

Joan delivered the message of the voices to Charles de Ponthieu, the country's weak leader: God had sent her to help him recover France from the English invaders. Even more amazing than her obedience was the result. Joan so impressed Charles and his court that they put the seventeen-year-old girl in charge of an army she led to significant military victories. Although the war continued, by July 1429 Joan was able to stand beside King Charles VII at his coronation.

On certain days during the war Joan felt particularly young, naive, inexperienced, and wilted. On her worst days, she wished she were a mere battlefield wallflower. Yet she found herself sustaining arrow wounds to the shoulder and leading the final charge. Girded by heaven's promptings, Joan withstood the blows. And, despite a crossbow bolt wound to the leg, she directed troops until the fighting ended, remembering the call. Joan presided at councils, sparred at battles, lead the army in victories ultimately reversing the tide of the war.

On May 23, 1430, Joan of Arc was given royal orders to withdraw. On horseback, parchment in hand, the scribbled *withdraw* seemed to jump off the page and punch her in the gut. Around her, a melee raged on in a frenetic fury of blood and fervor: swords slashing, wounds bleeding, lives ending. Wanting confirmation of the order, Joan gazed heavenward. She listened for God's voice and only heard wind and the terror of men dying. Then, even as she stood at the front lines, she breathed and made space enough to hear a whispered *yes* float in on the tail of the wind. *It is time for your mission to end.* The directive was as temperate and gracious, an unmistakable voice.

Joan turned to her ragamuffin troops, "Retreat, I command you. Withdraw and retreat," as she hollered, she was stricken by surprise confidence at her own words. She felt as if an apple were stuck in her throat. If she didn't cry she thought she'd surely choke. Painfully, Joan gulped down the urge to bawl while watching hundreds of men — bloodied and weighed down by the bludgeoning of war — fall out.

*They're taking my orders,* she thought. Joan felt as stunned that they were obeying now as she had been during the first battle. She found it ironic and affirming that because she'd been willing to do the outlandish, listen to a voice, so were her men.

Undaunted, Joan stood on the field until the last soldier was safe. In that place of honor, she was captured by the Burgundians, Frenchmen who had sided with the British. Later, she was sold to the English government and brought to a trial that tempted her to deny the voices, to deny herself.

Joan sat in the courtroom facing her accusers on a diminutive, solitary footstool, which made her feel, all at once, unbalanced and alone. She studied the faces of her judges, Bishop Cauchon and the Inquisitor of Paris, searching for a speck of mercy, understanding, open-mindedness. They sat in high-backed, gold-gilded thrones of pietistic condemnation, bloodthirsty for a public execution.

Her trial began on February 21, 1431, and lasted for six weeks. Joan was questioned for up to six hours each day in a room hung with ornate tapestries, many featuring the Mary holding Baby Jesus. The room's decor blessed and held the girl, comforting her in God's presence. Tapestries helped Joan summon the wisdom and grace of God's voice. Light dancing on stained-glass portraits of the Resurrection gave her hope. Reliquary icons that dotted tables became perfect focal points. And, though she could not read, psalters pregnant with Latin phrases silently lauded and encouraged Joan. She loved and needed the symbols of the church to bolster her faith, to remind her of the audacious voices during this desperate time.

Dozens of priests bordered the room. The first few days, Joan expected them to be sympathetic to her cause, to validate what otherwise was absurd but for God's great power. She remembered the sweet refreshment she'd found from priests during private confession as a child. They always honored the weight of her words and provided lightness to her spirit. *These* judgmental men of the cloth, apoplectic with hatred for her, merely squinted cold, bladelike eyes and wagged fat, balding heads.

When Joan was not under interrogation in the room of adornments, she was in a dark cell where she feared sexual attack by male guards, was refused sacraments, chained to her bed, and forced to sleep in fetters. *What kind of war criminal do you think I am?* she wondered. *Fettered? Even as I sleep?*

During the proceedings Bishop Cauchon frequently licked his index finger turning page after parchment page in a book of religious law. Joan found it amusing that the bishop never came to the trial prepared, with pages marked, arguments planned. He seemed to randomly select passages and craft nonsensical accusations directed at her, using the words as a shaky and unreliable base.

The bishop finally rested his index finger on a decree. He read it aloud in a particularly annoying, accusatory yet nasal and squeaky way, "God's voice seldom comes in concrete, organic, humanlike forms. It is the devil's messages that are specific, recountable, sensual." Joan recognized that the nauseatingly pious prig was about to set one of his many traps for her.

"Tell me, Joan, when you saw St. Michael, did he appear naked, or was he clothed?"

With youthful ardor and a quick wit Joan replied, "Do you think God could not afford to dress him?"

A couple of priests held back a chortle, their first and only sympathetic gesture. Joan smiled like a gamer at checkmate.

A bright-red cardinal lit on a branch outside the window. It was as if her voices were saying, *Nicely done . . . way to be strong, hang in there . . . hold on to your sass and spark, Joan.*

"Guilty of heresy," squealed the bishop in a blast of nasal words.

He followed this with an ecclesiastical evil eye because she testified she could smell, hear, see, describe her voices. In his interpretation of church law Joan had overphysicalized the saints, and in that imaginal act, turned them from spirits to demons.

Frustrated that Joan wouldn't buckle under pressure, the accusers started a wrestling match over Joan's convictions regarding church authority. "Do you not believe that you owe submission to God's church on earth, that is, to our Lord the Pope, to the cardinals, archbishops, and other prelates of the church?"

Joan loved her church. For a second she considered asking the voices for help in answering this line of questioning. Instead, and without pause, she answered, "Yes, but God must be served first."

Suddenly Joan realized that the voices had accomplished their work in her. She had listened to and followed their absurd call. Thanks to them, she'd developed a strong, passionate, divinely inspired voice of her own. Her answers poured out as freely as rain in April. Convictions shone as sure as sun.

"Is that your *final* answer?" squeaked the judge.

"You won't have another answer from me," said Joan, the corners of her mouth slightly raised, shoulders leavened.

The wound-red judge leaned forward, wiping sweat from his upper lip with a swooping sleeve of priestly gown; his voice shrieked in a fever-pitched bellow, "Do you consider yourself to be in a state of God's grace?"

Joan knew, down to the heavy pit in her stomach, that this line of questioning would be her ultimate undoing. Should she say *yes*, on her head more heresy would be heaped for claiming to know the mind of God. Should she say *no* . . . that answer held its own obvious and perilous predicament.

Joan didn't blink; she steeled herself in her seat, and answered, "If I am not, may God put me there; if I am, may He keep me there."

On the thirtieth of May 1431, a friar visited Joan's cell. Flimsy evidence and a twisted proof-text of Joan's words had been braided into a death sentence. The friar broke bread and poured wine. He anointed Joan's head with perfumed oil, "Yea though you walk through the valley of the shadow of death . . ." Last rites.

Joan whispered, "Am I going to be killed . . . tortured? How will I die? Decapitation? Incineration? I'd rather have my head chopped off seven times, than be burned!" She swallowed the bread and left her cell for the last time.

Guards shaved Joan's head and covered it with a cap, mocking: *heretic, apostate, idolater.* They forced her into a dress — which had been dipped in sulfur — then into the executioner's cart. Her penultimate sight was the scaffold and sticks. The last was of a golden crucifix, held by her friend and confessor, Martin Ladvenu. Arms shaking, he kept it directly before Joan's eyes as she burned.

"I forgive you. Will you forgive me?" Joan said as flames stripped her of the dress.

Then, in a flurry of last words, "My voices *did* come from God and everything that I have done was by God's order . . . Hold the crucifix up before my eyes so I can see it until I die. *Jesus, Jesus, Jesus!"*

> *God said to His people, Israel:*
> *Do not fear, for I have redeemed you;*
> > *I have summoned you by name; you are mine.*
> *. . . When you walk through the fire,*
> > *you will not be burned;*
> > *the flames will not set you ablaze.*
> *Since you are precious and honored in my sight,*
> *and because I love you.*

> (ISAIAH 43:1-2, 4 NIV)

## AFTER THE STORY

Joan of Arc's mission had exposed her strengths and weaknesses: genius, of stubborn will and fiery tenacious spirit; yet a peasant girl of 17 living during the autumn of the Middle Ages. Joan intuitively knew the way others would perceive her. It came as no surprise when learned men, political rulers, even kings would call Joan a witch, a sorceress, a woman "susceptible to illusions." Her interior monologue disagreed. Joan believed that she was chosen, special, called by God to do something completely confounding and spectacular.

Though she was convicted of heresy and died at the stake, ultimately Joan of Arc was cleansed, pardoned, and canonized by the Catholic Church. With her death, a meteoric power was unleashed. The crater of her bravery even to the point of death, still dimples the world today.

# PONDERINGS FOR THE HEART:
## *Reflecting on God's Love*

Joan listened to voices bearing an unlikely—even absurd—life mission. Today women may hear "voices" urging us to follow our bliss, live outside of our sphere of comfort, do something creative, outrageous, wild. Our voices may come in the form of an inspiring comment from one of our friends that sticks with us unwaveringly. Or they may come in a magazine advertisement for a writing workshop or a spiritual retreat. They may even show up in a dream or through an idea that pops into our heads during a walk or vacation or refueling at the local coffee shop. As we listen we wait, continue to listen more, and enter into a process of discerning and contemplating what we have heard—that meets the test of Scripture.

1. Do you see any of Joan of Arc in yourself? Is it easy or somewhat difficult for you to acknowledge and honor inner-promptings? In light of those questions, consider the following quote from Sue Monk Kidd,

> *On my thirtieth birthday, I walked into the kitchen of my brick house in South Carolina and announced to my husband and two children, "I'm going to become a writer." That was my annunciation. In a kitchen. To a two-year-old and a five-year-old and a husband who was trying to get them to eat their cereal. My plan was earnest but highly unlikely. I lovingly refer to it now as my "great absurdity." We should all have one or two of those in our lives—a hope so extravagant it seems completely foolish and implausible. I'd studied nursing and worked during my twenties in hospitals on surgical, pediatric, and obstetrical units, even spending one summer as a public health nurse. I didn't know anything about creative writing or whether I had any ability for it. All I had was the impulse and passion of my heart.*

2. Describe a time when you received a "divine nudge." How did it come to you? Did you deny or listen to a "still, small voice"? What happened

as a result? What did you learn from the experience? What would happen if you listened to God's nudges more often?

3. Who or what do you perceive as "authority" in your life? In other words, what voice dictates the story of your life? Do other people's opinions shape and advise your behavior? Have you ever gone against the grain of hierarchal expectation, either your own or others? How did this feel? What encourages you to continue to "authorize" your life? What discourages?

4. Do you believe God's presence can be experienced in tangible, concrete, sensory ways? Through sunsets and songs, words and water? Does God speak to you through Scripture? Questioning? Calling? Beckoning? Enticing? What does God's voice sound like to you? Describe it.

5. What "great absurdity" is beckoning you? What makes this "call" feel impossible, untimely, or unrealistic? What would happen if you entertained pieces or parts of this absurdity now? How can you better honor Jesus "tugs" on your spirit?

# HEARTBEATS:
## Acting on God's Love

1. Consider if you are in a place where you're waiting, expecting, or needing to hear God's divine voice. Or, consider if hearing a heavenly harkening might freak you out. Be where you are and offer yourself a gentle grace for the heart space you occupy.

   If you're open for a word: Take a walk, or sit on a pillow or favorite chair. Breathe deeply. Quiet your inner dialogue in order to open yourself to a new voice: God's voice impressing your heart.

2. Has God been offering you a great absurdity? Asking you to do something outrageous, unexpected, surprising? Is it about a new career path, a relationship, a call to serve in a new way? Listen. Make a list of steps that might help you take a risk in following the voice.

3. Joan was judged and condemned by her church authorities. What is your experience with church? How has your church supported your faith journey and your sense of God's love for you? Have you had any experiences where you did not feel supported? Do you have feelings and experiences that need to be resolved? Or is there a need for reconnection? Repair? Healing?

4. And, have you experienced the church itself as a place of healing and grace? Describe a time where you've felt God's love because of an experience in church.

5. Write a letter to yourself. Use a voice that you long to hear. What words of encouragement, strength, hope, wisdom, love, guidance, forgiveness, blessing, do you need for your journey? Let the letter come from that hidden place that knows exactly what you need. For a designated length of time — perhaps for a week — read it every morning before you roll out of bed to face the day. Then, if you're inspired, write a letter to a friend who may need your voice of love, forgiveness, affirmation, encouragement.

*We have always needed someone like her, someone who can disinfect us of our disreputable or petty tendencies. If we can love her, then we are not a people who hate women. If we can call her death a triumph . . . we [don't] measure success only by what seems to work. If we devote ourselves to her, we are higher creatures than the way we live our lives suggests. We need her as the heroine of our better selves.*

— MARY GORDON

# CHAPTER 7

# Julian of Norwich Imagines Beyond Herself

## THE FACTS

NAME: Julian of Norwich. This was not her given name but the Christian name St. Julian's Church at Conisford in Norwich, England, gave her. Since her given name is not known, we'll call her Kristyan prior to her church naming.

DATE OF BIRTH: November 8, 1342

DATE OF DEATH: c. 1416

OTHERWISE KNOWN AS: Dame Julian of Norwich, Lady Julian, Juliana

SUMMARY: Little is known about Julian of Norwich's life. Some believe she came from poor means, others think that she was the offspring of great wealth. It has been speculated that Julian was a Benedictine nun of the house of Carrow, near Norwich. Or that she was a young mother whose husband and children were victims of the plague (which ravaged her town three times during her life). The most information about her can be found only in her adored writings: *A Book of Showings* or *Sixteen Revelations of Divine Love*.

An excruciating seven-day illness and near-death experience after which Dame Julian reported she had 16 visions — or *showings* — inspired her to become a writer. (Less dire circumstances have inspired others to pick up the pen!) Her joyous, compassionate words about the ineludible love of God touched the lives of many who felt oppressed by a dogmatic church and their morbid medieval circumstances.

ॐ TRIVIA: Dame Julian was an *Anchorite* (or *Anchoress*). After her experience of visions, she vowed to live in a one-room cell walled to St. Julian Church in Norwich. Interestingly enough, the word *anchorite* comes from the Greek *anachorein*, which means "to withdraw" or "make room." Juliana "made room" for 43 years, living a contemplative life of prayer, study, and writing at length about 16 visions. (In the twelfth and thirteenth centuries 92 anchoresses resided in England.)

ॐ NOTABLE: *Sixteen Revelations of Divine Love* is the oldest extant book written in English by a woman.

ॐ QUOTABLE: "All shall be well, and all shall be well, and all manner of thing shall be well."

— JULIAN OF NORWICH

A MAXIM OF THE STORY: Julian — using her imagination — looked beyond herself and through the disparaging circumstances of her day toward a God who is immutably compassionate, gracious, and overflowing with a mysterious, uncontainable love. She realized that God helps us hold the tensions of life (the woe and weal) in a palm of goodness.

In May of 1373, he slunk into her life like a shadowy thief breaking in to ransack a home. His morose, nefarious, black presence was undeniable. He revealed himself, at first, in the worst migraine headache imaginable. With even the slightest movement of her head, Kristyan felt as if her skull would split. Barely able to stay balanced on a stool, pressing a cool wet cloth to her forehead, she begged, "Help me, God! You, who can use mere mustard seeds to move mountains; bring relief from this inexorable pain." When the prayers seemed to go unanswered, Kristyan drew a cup of water and tried to reason away the presence of her predator, *Perhaps I'm dehydrated.* She took a long, languid gulp. Her body welcomed the cold liquid the way the lonely welcome a friend.

For a peaceful moment it seemed as though the plague had fled. Then chills and fever came, rapaciously forcing the recently widowed Kristyan to the floor. Her sore knees intuitively curled to her chest in an effort to soothe tumultuous waves of nausea. She circled achy arms around her knees. *Has the plague that took my husband and son now come for me?* she asked the heavens from a dusty corner of her humble home near Norwich, England.

At that precise moment a single slant of light infiltrated the room. It was so bright Kristyan couldn't stand it. She covered her head with a corner of billowy beige blouse and drifted into a sleep bordering on unconsciousness.

Two days passed. Kristyan's mother, who had stopped by for a casual visit, found her daughter still slumped on the floor in the corner. Kristyan shrank back in pain at the sound of her mother's footsteps. They sounded alien, vibrating in earsplitting oscillatory madness. Mother's frantic, breathy voice broke in, "Dear . . . one . . . what . . . what's . . . wro— . . . wrong?" Words seemed to bounce and echo about the room pelting thirty-year-old Kristyan in the forehead and inner ear.

The sick woman couldn't respond to Mother. The ability to move or speak had been sucked out like the last slurp of soup in a homeless child's bowl. In a daze, she felt limp head and torso being lifted, then flopping. Mother adjusted, then held the rag doll-limp body. Her familiar arms and legs formed a human cradle, holding, rocking, protecting Kristyan from the cold, hard ground. For a moment, safe in the arms of Mother, Kristyan rested in calm, her breathing resonating with her mother's metronomic lulling rhythm. She was held.

Suddenly, she heard a woman sobbing. Confused, Kristyan couldn't tell if it was her own cries or her mother's. "Wake up . . . wake up . . . I beseech you, wake up!" The voice of her mother resounded. Words charged into the room, shattering the peace, then dropping quickly like stones in water. Kristyan tried to raise stubborn eyelids, but they were cemented shut. As if in slow motion she felt the older woman grab her arms in a vice-like grip, then wildly shake her. "Wake up . . . wake up . . . I beg of you, awake!" Kristyan couldn't steady her head. It drooped and rolled augmenting throbbing headache and nausea.

In spite of its ill effects, the shaking produced a modicum of sentience. Eyes cracked open so that Kristyan could see distorted images: a paned window, the face of her mother, and, on the kitchen table, the empty cup from which she'd drank. She also caught a glimpse of hands and arms — mere days ago flushed with exuberance and life — now turned a sallow grey. With a voice raspy from lack of use, Kristyan weakly extended an arm for Mother to see and asked, "Plague?"

Mother didn't answer. She didn't have to. Kristyan knew that her question had named the thief. In rasps that stopped and started, she repeated his moniker in mantra-like fashion, emphasizing every letter, "*Plague . . . death . . . I curse you, plague!*"

Wiping away the start of tears, Mother draped one of Kristyan's arms over her shoulder and dragged the seemingly lifeless woman to bed. In bed, Kristyan regained more awareness. For some reason the time of year — just after Easter — began to crystallize in her mind. She could almost smell the sweetness of the lilies circling the altar at St. Julian's. *A strange time to die,* she thought. *It would've made more sense for me to go during the dark of Lent. Or better, on Good Friday.* In a demanding mental tone she looked to God, asking, *Am I dying, Lord?* She wanted to know, and she wanted to know *now.* That way she could start preparing for the long hello of heaven and her final farewell to everything she'd known thus far.

God was silent.

Gideon and his fleece flooded into Kristyan's consciousness. Like the curious judge, she wanted to know the future, the fallout, the end. With all the misfortune that had befallen her, Kristyan had every intention of setting out as many fleeces as she needed. *There's nothing wrong with that,* she figured. *It's up to God if He answers or not.*

Mother lifted Kristyan's head and slid her arm beneath her daughter's neck in the beginning of an embrace. As the arm brushed Kristyan's skin, she realized that the back of her neck was an inferno of heat and pain. "What is this on the back of your neck, my dear?" Mother asked.

Kristyan couldn't respond; but she began to notice a half dozen telltale bumps produced by the plague that grew about her body. This was not merely her imagination. In a rapidly boiling disgust, she thought, *Curse you for making your ghastly, ravaging residence beneath my neck, under my arms . . . between my knees!* As if in retort, a nightmarish remembrance popped into her mind. In it Kristyan saw the same ghastly growths on her husband, William, and their son, Nicholas. Monstrously they grew, becoming black as obsidian, then splitting open, spilling blood, putrid pus, and the lives of their hosts.

On the third day of illness, Benedictine sisters from the house of Carrow circled Kristyan's bed to pray. They were the same resolute and ebullient hens who'd cleaned house, made meals, and interceded for Kristyan when she'd lost her loved ones to the plague. Today their intercessory chattering overlapped and played off one another like bunnies in a glade, like handbells in church, "Lord, we beseech You to heal this faithful woman . . ." "In Your resurrected power . . . and goodness . . . renew her life." "We have walked with her through Lent's tomb. Please now, restore her health by the promise of Eastertide." "Yes," came the others' whispered affirmation. "Yes, yes, restore her health, we pray."

During and after the prayers, some of the sisters sang songs of

Easter and triumph and hope, *Gloria in excelsis Deo, gloria in excelsis, in excelsis Deo.* Others paced — really strutted — scratching at the floor with the soles of their shoes: hens in the hen house. One sister sat beside the bed, near Kristyan's head, praying the rosary. *Our Father who art in heaven, hallowed be thy name . . .* To Kristyan, the sister's voice was all at once fortissimo and muted. Sounds and senses were a cloud of blur to her. Prayer beads clicked together as loud as a sonic boom. Consonants and vowels danced and melted and dropped like cotton falling to the dusted floor.

From her waist down, Kristyan felt numb, paralyzed. It seemed as if her body was an empty vessel quickly filling with liquid paralysis. Fear overtook her as she imagined the level of numbness reaching her torso, arms, neck, and face. She felt as if she was being suffocated and began desperately coughing. She was stuck, a prisoner inside herself. The rosary-saying sister's mantic voice pierced through Kristyan's fear. *Thy kingdom come. Thy kingdom come. Thy kingdom come . . . Thy will be done on earth as it is in heaven . . .* As the nun raced round the beads, the cough subsided and another memory began racing through Kristyan's garbled mind.

The imaginary memory was collage-like, with overlapping, intensely colorful, graphic images. It defied the laws of nature and was particularly rhapsodic. In the memory, Kristyan imagined four depictions of herself: as a little girl playing in a grassy field, an adolescent sleeping, a young wife kissing her husband, and new mother sitting on a kitchen stool nursing her newly born infant. Each of the selves in the very midst of their activities and settings sat — strangely enough — in a pristine row on an oaken pew in St. Julian's Church of Norwich. White, sugary, aromatic lilies and a victorious hymn made it obvious to her that the memory contained the glory of every Easter Kristyan had experienced in her entire life. Each Kristyan somehow, graciously, looked beyond herself to God, needed God, talked to God, saw God.

In an almost mechanical, synchronized fashion four Kristyans' mouths began to pray, *Heavenly Father, I ask You for three wishes . . . graces from You. You know I believe, but some days I need proof. I want to see, hear, smell the reality of You. So, first, I ask to see You in bodily form. You parted the sea for Moses, dropped Jericho's walls, gave Samson indomitable strength. All*

*I ask is to see You wrapped in skin. You made my eyes. I beg of You to allow them to see — really see — You, Jesus!*

*My second desire, and I know it sounds raving mad, is to come close enough to death (during my thirtieth year of life) that I could . . .* Before the Kristyans could finish their second request and begin the third, she imagined God's laughter interrupted . . . round, frolicking, lower than bass, packed with love and amusement at Kristyan's medieval melodramatics. Though it contained the power of the sea. There was not a drop of malevolence in it, only a maternal kind of love that yearns to bless and gift and nurture.

In her disoriented condition, Kristyan couldn't tell if the laughter was a present phenomenon or part of the remembering. Either way, something in her soul found it both cosmically weird and wondrous that God laughed as she lay dying. *Perhaps God is laughing at death,* she hazily considered in her imagining.

With persistence that pulled Kristyan back to the present, she whispered, "Lift me up . . . support my head . . . so . . . I . . . may be . . . more . . . free to be close to God," she said. Mother, with the help of the sisters, lifted Kristyan, steadied her wobbly head and placed cloths on her brow. A trio of sisters bustled about the room bumping into one another, quibbling. To Kristyan they were a blur of black and white. She could only make out a few of their words: *Her eyes . . . fixed . . . Call Father . . . holy oil . . . never coming back . . . Extreme unction . . .*

Within the hour the parson came. Kristyan greedily inhaled the fresh air and sunshine that clung to his smock as he entered her room. With heavy breath, authority, and kindness, the man of God set a cross before Kristyan's lifeless eyes. She could feel something warm and slick on her forehead. It smelled curiously of olives and frankincense. The priest slathered the substance up and down, side to side and said, "Through this holy anointing, may the Lord in His love and mercy help you with the grace of the Holy Spirit." In the moment, it didn't dawn on Kristyan that she was living the answer to one of the prayers — the second in the trio — that she'd prayed for her entire lifetime. Death was near.

Last rites administered, the priest reached under the blanket to take Kristyan's hand. Hard as she tried, though, she couldn't feel his holy touch. The room suddenly became still and silent as snow. Mother's hand hovered over her daughter's head for what seemed like eons. Then, gently, Mother used a shaky index finger to close Kristyan's eyes for what she thought was the last time.

In the days that followed Kristyan vacillated between life and death. On the seventh morning, vigilant Mother declared, "Look! Light is pouring from her face . . . she's smiling." And a day filled with sixteen visions began.

The man's face was ashen yet kind. Though He was obviously dying, His weary eyes shone with lingering sparks of ineffable love. Something about the gentleman gave Kristyan a lump in the throat. Gazing at Him caused fluttering wings to sprout at the edges of her heart. For the first time in five years the death of her husband and son became a shadow instead of a dark endless night. Kristyan's compulsion to stare at the man obscured the peculiarity of His presence. It didn't even cross her mind to ask who He was, where He came from or what He was doing in her vision. She was captivated: lost in His curiously lovely face. Though He looked nothing like her husband, something about him reminded Kristyan of her Will. *Maybe it's the kindness in the corners of His eyes,* she wondered.

In her imagination she examined every line and contour of His face as if it were an obscure and holy text. It seemed that in His eyes and cheeks and lips and hair were words — answers — to her deepest questions, to the mysteries of the universe. She began examining the dying man's hair. It was a tangle of curls and clotting blackish blood. Woven amidst the wild nest of hair, she spied a thorn-covered vine. Copious amounts of warm crimson blood flowed from beneath the barbed circlet.

The wings fell off her heart. The heart rent in two. Kristyan reached for the dying man. But as she reached the bleeding man fell into a starless night; and she got the sickening sensation of plummeting into an equally dark and boundless chasm. The urge to help, place a cloth and pressure on His wounds, encourage blood to congeal, offer a cold cup of water, was tenacious. With her hand forced to her side, the man appeared again directly before Kristyan, mere feet away. Kristyan was close enough to see whiskers, numerous abrasions, and popped blood vessels on His cheeks and neck. As soon as she reached out to help, to eradicate his predicament, the farther away he moved. An evil darkness rampant with demons — an obtuse barrier of evil spirits, for miles and days — seemed to keep her from the man in desperate need of help.

Frozen by impotence to help, Kristyan began to realize that what she saw had already occurred. *No matter what I do, I can't help, or change, or relieve this pain. It has already happened!* Slowly, skeptically, she looked out of the corner of her eye to the right. A woman with long brown hair, streaked in grey, knelt sobbing. No one needed to tell Kristyan that the woman was the mother of the dying man. With no hesitation this time, Kristyan whipped her head to the left where she saw another weeping woman and a grieving younger man.

In the vision and in her bed Kristyan shouted, "Blessed be the Lord!" As the words rang round the room, stirring those still keeping vigil, Kristyan was suddenly aware that all of her pain had been remitted. Fourteen more visions materialized that afternoon. Many were corporeal sights of Christ's passion. Others were pictures of God in an instant, revealing a compassion, unshakable goodness, and divine love. In some of the visions she imagined inanimate objects like garments of clothing or hazelnuts.

The hazelnut rolled round the palm of Kristyan's hand, small, hard, and brown. *This seems to be a wasted, bizarre vision. I'd rather gaze on the face of God again,* she thought. *This tiny thing might as well fall out of my grasp, roll into a crack, or disintegrate beneath someone's boot.*

"*You hold everything that has ever been made in your hand,*" said a familiar voice.

It was God again. The first few times she'd audibly heard the divine voice, Kristyan was mortified. Its timbre and resonance shook her to the very bone. But, she was getting used to the voice, even becoming comfortable questioning it, "*How can this tiny, insignificant thing be everything ever made?*"

*It is and always will be.* The answer.

*That's a quizzical answer,* she thought, rolling the nut between both of her pointer and thumb, then her palms, warming it. *I could crush this lil' nut right now if I wanted. It's awfully small, God, isn't it?*

*The universe is small . . . compared to me. I hold it, and because of my love it is sustained forever.*

Something flashed in Kristyan's imagination: a spark of epiphany. As quickly as it flickered it was gone and so was the nut.

Late during the day of visions and active imagination, Kristyan caught another glimpse of the dying man's face. It was caked with drying blood. The contempt of persecutors, like a distorted reflection in a murky pond, shone on his woeful countenance. Kristyan's heart fluttered with compassion and anticipation. *It is Him again!* From the bed, Kristyan leaned toward the face trying to get a better look. *Maybe if I see Him again* all *of my grief over Will and Nicholas will vanish.*

The image was too blurry, obscured by shadows. Daylight from her window and light within the vision were waning. "God, please shine more light so that I can see better," she pleaded.

The answer was clear and iconic, *If I wished to show you more, child, I would. Besides, you need no light but Me.*

The next night, Kristyan had one last vision of the once dying man. By the look of His face, the anguish was a distant memory. This time, skin was clean and shiny. He smelled of soap and spoke vibrantly, alive with joy and story. She sat beside Him on a grassy hill where they enjoyed laughter, silence, and a caress of breeze.

With jokes, profundity, and infinite patience, He answered Kristyan's questions about suffering and loss and the magical ways God's love brings right from wrong, mercy after mourning, beauty out of brokenness. She asked about Will and their son. He offered the perfect words.

In that moment, Kristyan noticed sun and stars and moon shining in the sky above the hill where they sat; and she did not wonder why.

By the time Kristyan's visions faded, her health had completely returned, and she reentered life as a widow living on the outskirts of Norwich. Irksome feelings surprised and entrapped her. It was much better on the mountaintop with Him in a vision-filled delirium. But, now she was stuck in the valley, awake to the messy quotidian realities of life. Most days, in the drudgery of it all, she told herself that the visions and epiphanies were psychological manifestations of her illness. Psychedelic hallucinations. Her spiritual perceptions began to wane like a flame nearing the end of its wick until Simeon, a spiritual seeker from a neighboring town, paid a visit. The second after he entered her home, Kristyan regretted letting the stranger in.

Sitting at the table near the corner where, mere days before, Kristyan slumped in a stupor, Simeon—hand shaking—spilt water from a tin cup. His eyes widened exposing clear, bright whites; his eyebrows rose unusually wide. He leaned forward in his seat, invading Kristyan's space. With a prying, fiercely nasal voice, he said, "The wind and the birds and my neighbors have been telling me that, during your near fatal illness, God visited you. Is this true?"

Kristyan pushed her stool away from the table. "It is true that I nearly died. But, the visions... ah, I was a raving lunatic... a madwoman under the fever and pain." Kristyan began to nervously laugh. The chortle surprised her and sickened her stomach the way curdled cream could.

Simeon added his hearty guffaw. The laugh was pure and round and wondrous. It made the curls in his hair bounce and shine light and dance. It softened her reticent heart and reminded her of someone. But, she couldn't remember who it was. When the laughter subsided, the man leaned back in his chair folding his arms above bulbous belly. His question was casual and pointed, "What did you see?"

Caught in the web of his directness, and having a sense that Simeon somehow knew what she had seen, Kristyan blurted, "I saw the face of Christ . . . He wore a crown of thorns . . . Blood flowed in profusion down his face." Then, caught up in the memory of it all, she slowed down, "His countenance heralded love as if it were a . . . as if it were a sonnet." She began to giggle uncomfortably.

The stranger sat transfixed in seriousness. Kristyan swallowed the nervous laugh. Shame bloomed in redness and heat on her cheeks. *He is taking me seriously . . . and with respect,* she thought.

Simeon rose and casually walked to the door. Poised to leave, he looked over his shoulder, "Thank you for entertaining me this afternoon. Your active imagination has helped you look beyond yourself and see God. Today you've told me exactly what I've been longing to hear for my entire life." Before leaving, the stranger winked, nodded, and smiled at his hostess with warm, bright, clandestine smile. "I bid you well and pray that you will talk to a priest about your visions."

When word of Kristyan's visions finally reached the archbishop, she had already decided to become Anchoress of St. Julian's Church of Norwich. Much like the epiphanies, though, the decision didn't come easily or without pain. For days before the ceremony to ordain Kristyan as an anchorite, she wondered if her choice was ill motivated.

It didn't help matters when Mother protested, "Sequestered living arrangements are not the only way to live a contemplative life, Kristyan."

"Living in the anchorhold will give me protection and care from the bishop," Kristyan argued. "Besides, becoming an anchoress is the only logical response to what I have seen . . . to the visions."

Mother held steadfast to her position, and though Kristyan appeared to be unwavering about a monastic life, daily doubts swirled and nested in her head and fickle heart. *Maybe I'm not cut out for this. I wish God would just tell me what to do. He wrote a plan on the wall, in almighty penmanship for Daniel. Why can't He do the same for me? Perhaps it is time for another fleece.*

Twisting about her bed during a late summer evening, she continued the internal debate, *Perhaps I'm just trying to hide from my former life . . . which is raving . . . because no matter where I go, my losses follow me like a wretched shadow.*

The bed linens were clammy and damp. So was Kristyan. No combination of mental or physical acrobatics brought comfort, peace, and closure. She tried to picture the 12-by-12-foot stone cell walled to St. Julian Church. It smelled like snow: cold and air-fresh and like stone. The floor was dusty and grey. No art hung on the walls. And there were only two small, paned windows. One faced the street. The other opened to the sanctuary so the inhabitant could participate in mass, receive the bread and wine.

Kristyan imagined herself eating, praying, sleeping, writing, *being* in the tiny room . . . permanently. As she saw herself writing and praying in the anchorhold, it was filled with light and a gentle breeze. A sense of warmth and freedom, companionship and assurance comforted her like the voice of a good friend. Without any warning, the image morphed, darkened. Suddenly, Kristyan was alone, trying to sleep in the finite cell. She was freezing. A claustrophobic clutch overtook her. Breathing became difficult. Her heart raced. She felt as if she had been buried alive.

Kristyan leapt from her bed, ran to the front door, threw it open, and ravenously drew in three long, deep breaths of England's intoxicating, moist midnight air. Before she realized what was happening a profusion of breath and words filled the space in front of her like stars in the sky, *If I go into the anchorhold, I'll never again be able to throw open my front door. It will be bricked shut. Forever. Never again will I run through fresh air, feel the wind in my hair and the sun on my face.* She sat on the front stoop, her head on her knees, shaking . . . weeping.

The last few leaves clung to almost bare calligraphic trees surrounding St. Julian's. Autumn ushered in winter as droves of Londoners were ushered into the church. Kristyan felt like a bride on her wedding day. In this moment, she was sure of her choice in the moment, but stood in knee-knocking fear that the reality of her commitment might not live up to her expectations. *Only by committing will I know*, she thought as she studied her cell's three simple furnishings: a bed, a chair, and a desk that would serve as kitchen table and library.

Outside, the bishop, dressed in black miter and cassock, stood beside a pile of dusty, megalithic bricks. His opulent Latin called the service to order and Kristyan to stand by the front door of the dwelling. With a bevy of priests assisting, the bishop directed a series of questions at Kristyan: *From this day forward do you vow to remain in this dwelling place until your corpse is removed by the church? Do you willingly take the vow of chastity, poverty, and obedience? Will you commit to keeping daily hours of prayer, study, and service as a spiritual advisor...?*

With each question that Kristyan answered affirmatively, the bishop placed an enormous stone in the doorway of the anchorhold. The priests provided mortar. With the addition of each brick, Kristyan simultaneously felt honored at her call and worried that she'd bolt, or scream under the oppressive claustrophobic tension of it all. Somehow, she made her vows with peace and a surprising sense of internal liberation.

At the *amen,* a minor arpeggio of notes and choral voices wafted through the stained glass windows of St. Julian's and into Kristyan's cell. The music was a requiem Mass: the traditional score used in masses for the dead and for ordaining anchorites. Mother was hysterical as each stone was added to the doorway. The funeral dirge accompaniment heightened her hysteria. From within the anchorhold, Kristyan blocked out the sound of Mother's protests. Instead she focused on the falling and rising melody of the requiem: a metaphor for the end to life as she knew it and the exciting, though uncertain, ushering in of a new day as she cast off cultural, personal, even familial expectations.

As Bishop fit the last stone into the top corner of the doorway, his voice got markedly louder and more majestic. The music crescendo supporting the sanctity of the moment, "From this day forward, the Anchoress of St. Julian's Church shall abide in these walls. Forevermore, she shall be known as Dame Julian of Norwich."

Julian smiled when she heard the new name. *It is finished,* she thought, but didn't say another word.

Most days in the anchorhold were patterned, predictable. Julian would rise for mass, spend an hour after that talking with God. Then, she'd run in place for a bit—get the brain oxygenated—write for a while, and have lunch (usually soup). A nap would typically follow, after which Julian would offer spiritual counsel through her "squint," the window on the street side, to anyone who wandered by and asked. The day ended with dinner, reflection, and an early bedtime. The best part of most days was when Julian made imaginal connections with God. The worst was the temptation to gossip, despair, and be lazy. "Life in here is a lot like life on the outside," she was known to say.

During her fifth December of contemplative living, on a particularly snowy day, Julian had no visitors. She sat at the squint for three hours watching fluffy tufts of white dance then settle on the grounds, villager's hats, the street, the market. Feeling lonely and useless on this snow globe day, she went to bed earlier than usual. As she drifted into the sweet spot of twilight dreaming, someone tapped her tiny window. *Maybe the snow is icing over,* she thought and rolled over.

*Tap, tap, tap-tap-tap.* The interruption was relentless. *Tap, tap, tap, tap, tap.* It was starting to sound intentional. Julian resentfully wrapped a woolen blanket about her shoulders and traipsed the short distance to the squint. Tentatively, she pulled back the curtain. A dark haired woman stood at the window, close enough for Julian to see her breath fog. Distress clinging to her face seemed to ease up at the sight of Julian.

"I do not typically keep window hours at this time," Julian said with a tender firmness in her voice.

The woman refused to leave, and launched into a heartrending story. Her husband and six children had all been stricken with this, the third epidemic outbreak of the plague in England. Word about their illness swirled through her town. Before the family succumbed to the illness, townspeople, trying to stop the infection from spreading, burned the woman's house to the ground with her loved ones still inside.

As the widow recounted the story, Julian considered sharing the prescient wisdom of one of her most vivid and compelling visions. In the vision she had experienced an otherworldly feeling of satisfaction. The satisfaction brought with it a sensation of secure peace, rest, and delight that inhabited her in a way that nothing in this world could have bothered her. The feeling passed, though. And, Julian was left alone. Feelings of weariness, fear, and oppression moved in. Then, the comfort and soul-rest returned. Once again, after the joy and comfort, pain, and aloneness returned. Shortly thereafter, security and safety lit a fire in the hearth of her heart. Again and again, about twenty times, the indwellers swapped places.

Julian wanted to tell the woman, her sister in suffering, that everyone is asked to hold the irreconcilable tensions of loss and love, despair and joy. Each woman, in her time, is comforted, then left on her own. Instead, Julian of Norwich leaned toward the dark-haired woman and listened to her story.

That night Julian sat to record the conversations and dualistic personal pendulum swings. Later, as she leaned back in her chair, she realized that only His hand can author and hold the tensions of weal and woe — good and bad — in our lives. Through it all, God alone is able to keep us safe. In the sorrow and joy He dwells within, tending the fire of perfect Love.

> *Writing teaches us to recognize when we have*
> *reached the limits of our language,*
> *and our knowing, and are dependent on our senses to "know*
> *for us."*
>
> — KATHLEEN NORRIS, THE CLOISTER WALK

## AFTER THE STORY

For 43 years that Julian of Norwich lived a cloistered life in the anchorhold of St. Julian's in Norwich. During her time there, she heard the stories of many who lost loved ones to the plague. Julian's joyous, compassionate writings wrapped a maternal receiving blanket of warmth and acceptance around a people besought with feelings of despair, and ecclesiastic words of legalism and judgment.

Hundreds visited Julian of Norwich, including contemporary mystic, Margery Kempes. Inspired by one of their visits, she wrote, "The Holy Spirit never prompts us to act unkindly; if He did He would be acting contrary to His own nature, for He is pure love." Today, people follow, revere, and turn to Julian's writings for comfort. As iconic and beloved as she is, Julian put it best, "By myself I am nothing at all, but in general, I am the *oneing* of love. For it is in this *oneing* that the life of all people exists." Classic Julian coined words, like *oneing*, that infuse theology, infuse our way of seeing one's self, God, and others. Her right brain helped her imagine a new way where, "The love of God creates in us such *oneing* that when it is truly seen, no person can separate themselves from another person." Even in an anchorhold.

An everyday, winsome woman turned profound Christian mystic and anchoress used her imagination to look past her life circumstances to contemplate and write about the ineffable love, joy, and compassion of God.

> *My definition of faith is "a widening of the imagination."*
>
> *If our imaginations are broadened enough, something that seems unbelievable to us can seem possible; and we can base our prayers that way.*
>
> *We broaden our prayer life by possibility thinking, not by negativism and legalism.*
>
> *I feel that a baptized, or redeemed, imagination is an imagination which is truly listening for God images.*
>
> — Luci Shaw

# PONDERINGS FOR THE HEART:
## Reflecting on God's Love

Julian was contained, isolated, alone, due to limiting factors in her life: the loss of loved ones, her illness, the time in history in which she lived, her anchorite cell. Each of us lives with isolating factors in our lives that disconnect us from self, others, and God. Julian's life and writings offer an assurance that God holds all things together, holds us just like that hazelnut. In engaging her creative, imaginative, intuitive faculties, Julian discovered the uniting, generative gifts of Jesus' love. As she widened her imagination, her faith in God's kindness and goodness and love grew.

Through all of her confinements, Julian used an active imagination to reach for God. Sometimes the right brain gets a bad rap in Christianity. But, God created our imaginative and intuitive capacities. And we, as women, often have large intuitive capacities that help us see the numinous: experiencing God through our rational minds *and* our God-given imaginations. If we follow in the spirit of Julian — even when we feel closed in by life circumstances — we can use our imaginations to reach beyond ourselves to God.

1. How do you feel about your imagination? Are you suspicious of it? Or do you tend to trust your gut, your imagination, your creative/intuitive side? Why or why not?

2. Have you experienced an image — like Julian's hazelnut — that may have helped you "see" God or understand Jesus better? Take some time to draw this image and write a journal entry or poem or free-association piece — with all the thoughts that come to your mind — about God.

3. Joan's identification of "voices" led her not into a convent cell or to a hermit's cave, like Julian, but, into battle. In your life do you feel God's love calling you more like Julian or Joan, or, perhaps you have other tugs from God. What do these feel like in your experience?

4. Several of God's girls — like Julian of Norwich did — changed their names, or were given new names, at turning points in their lives. Do you like your name or your nickname? What is the significance or meaning behind your name? What does your name mean to you? Does it fit who you are and who you want to be? If you were to rename yourself, what name would you choose? Why?

# HEARTBEATS:
## Acting on God's Love

1. When Julian was sick, and when she was in her cell, she experienced visions in her imagination, which allowed her to see and understand God more clearly.

   Take a moment to consider what images help you see God more clearly, connect you to the divine. Perhaps page through a magazine and notice images that attract you. Tear out these images. Arrange them in collage form on a table, or even paste them on a poster. As you study the images as representative of aspects of God, consider the following questions:

   If these images could talk, what would they tell me?

   What would I answer?

   Do these images convey something about my life?

   Are there insights about my connection to God, self, or others represented in the images gathered here?

2. Julian was set apart, literally locked in a cell in order to connect with God, to hear Jesus' voice. Is there a place that you can go to just *be?* Maybe it's a retreat house, the bathtub, the forest preserve, the library. When you have time, go there with no agenda other than considering Psalm 46:10, *Be still and know that I am God.*

> *Our contemporary mystics*
> *are the astrophysicists, the cellular biologists,*
> *the physicists who study quantum mechanics,*
> *for they are dealing with the nature of being itself.*
> — MADELEINE L'ENGLE

# CHAPTER 8

# Pocahontas Dreams God's Dreams

In this work of creative nonfiction, cultural traditions portrayed are based on the author's research. Any variance from fact is unintentional.

## THE FACTS

NAME: Matoaka (birth name), Pocahontas (childhood nickname), Lady Rebecca Rolfe (baptized name)

DATE OF BIRTH: Sometime around 1597

DATE OF DEATH: c. 1617 (at about 21 years of age)

OTHERWISE KNOWN AS: Indian Princess, the First Lady of America, Mother of Us All, Ambassador Between the Indians and American Colonists

SUMMARY: Pocahontas lived in *Werowocómoco*, a town of the native People, smack in the middle of the *tsenacommacah*. This territory, *tsenacommacah*, was located within modern-day Virginia's tidewater region geographically. By lineage and training, Pocahontas was a *Beloved Woman*, a spiritual guide, or wise, intuitive woman in her clan. Even as a small child, her opinion about tribal matters was revered. The pinnacle moment in her life occurred when her people captured Englishman John Smith, and slated him for execution. In an act of mercy, she spared his life, indicating that he should be "adopted" as a son of the *Powhatan* tribe. Later, Pocahontas was baptized; married Englishman John Rolfe; gave birth to a son, Thomas; and traveled to England.

TRIVIA: Pocahontas's tribe, the Mattaponi, belonged to a tribal alliance with 35-plus Native American nations. The alliance was known as *Powhatan* (literally translated, "People of the Dream-Vision"). The root, *powa* is difficult to translate. Its literal meaning is "dream." But, it connotes a divine power to heal, see, connect with the mysteries of the universe, with all that's sacred. Many spiritually significant words of the *Powhatan* people share the same root: *apowa* (dream-vision), *powwow* (we dream together), *powagan* (spiritual mentor or guide).

NOTABLE: "She was able to dream of two very different worlds coexisting and collaborating together in peace."

— Q'ORIANKA KILCHER

QUOTABLE: The Bible believed in dreams. It seems strange how much there is in the Bible about dreams. There are . . . some sixteen chapters in the Old Testament and four or five in the New in which dreams are mentioned . . . The emphasis upon dreams that we find in the Bible is equally prominent in the early church. Every major fixture of the early Christian Church through the time of St. Augustine cites dreams as an important way in which God spoke to people.

— JOHN A. SANFORD

A MAXIM OF THE STORY: *Pocahontas experienced God's love first in her dreams (apowa); next in living out her dream by playing a catalytic role in the "rebirth, salvation" of John Smith. In an unexpected climactic twist-of-life, the people Pocahontas saved—the English—ironically became instruments for an enlarged and deepened spiritual reality in her own life (as she encountered the Christ in faith).*

The *quioccosan* (Great House) was quieted in the sacredness and expectation of the moment. A fire danced large, crimson and crackling, circled by hundreds of *sunk* and *sunkskaa* (wise men and women). Phantasmagorical smoke created an ashy serpentine on its journey to the opening in the ceiling of the large hut. Flanking the fire, in a great square, four enormous poles held up the roof. Each was painted red on one side, black on the other. Tops of the poles came to life with the carved faces of a dragon, bear, eagle, and wild-eyed man.

It was the day of the Powhatan Alliance's Great Council. A particularly young, sinewy *sunk* stood by the fire. Light flickered on his bare arms and chest. It sparkled off copper chains and ringlets hanging from holes in his ears. From the bottom hole in his left ear hung a green and yellow snake about a half-yard long. The snake wriggled its head toward the Indian's face, seeming to give him a foreboding kiss on the lips.

At that precise moment, the wisest oldest *sunkskaa*, a woman called the Bringer of Prophecy, entered from the east. All eyes turned toward the wise old woman. She wore a cloak of smooth, white deer hide and matching dress adorned with copper beading. Black geometric tattoos on her hands, legs, and face appeared to walk about her skin in the flickers of fire. Her long, black hair was ornamented with gray, indicating wisdom. Her face, creased calligraphic with lines from sunshine and age, was heavy with news and story. She approached the flames and walked in slow circles about the fire, her moccasins liberating dusty earth.

The Bringer of Prophecy began to tell a story. Her voice was low and majestic in timbre, "Sky Woman bent over the hole where the Tree of Many Lights once lived. As she looked into the Great Hole, her husband heaved a Great Push, sending Sky Woman end over end into the abyss . . ."

Members of the sacred Powhatan assemblage nodded knowingly as they listened to one of their tribe's archetypal myths: *The Woman Who Fell from the Sky*. They knew it to be the story of woman as progenitor of life, of creation, of new beginnings, of love after loss, of redemption.

There was a peace and sense of home in the familiarity of the often-told narrative. It warmed like the fire and was undergirded with radiant anticipation. Anticipation about why the Bringer of Prophecy was telling their tale on this day.

Some of the sunkskaa, with tongues flailing, let out high-pitched cries that pulsated in smoky air. Their enthusiasm added to the allure and enchantment of the story. With rhythmic cadence to her words, the old prophet continued in her round mellow alto, "As Sky Woman fell, she grabbed whatever she could: soil, tree roots, bits of corn and seed embedded in soil. She fell and fell and fell. She fell into Forever. Into the darkness, into the deep she descended. Swan, with feathers as white as snow, made a nest of wings to break Sky Woman's fall. Gently Swan placed Sky Woman on the back of Great Turtle."

Logs on the fire burned to gray ashen dust. The myth continued, filled with a cast of surprising and symbolic creatures. The Bringer of Prophecy told how Sky Woman used mud that had collected on her body and in her hair during the fall to create a resting place. She described tenacious toads and otters helping with the work. And then, in a climactic ending, the old prophet told of Sky Woman bearing children who became new hope for the future.

Precisely as the Bringer of Prophecy spoke the last word of her story, a young woman who — from her earth-shatteringly beauteous face appeared to be from the Mattaponi tribe — entered the east door. She wore hand-strung freshwater pearls about her neck and a deerskin dress. In her arms she held a tiny pearl of a baby. Immediately everyone in the assembly sat in a hushed expectancy, knowing that the story was told in honor of this baby. Knowing that, today, the babe would receive a name somehow tying her to the tale.

The baby wailed as New Mother handed her to the Bringer of Prophecy. "This baby will be called Matoaka," the old woman's voice was full with promise and prediction. The papoose newly dedicated by story, quieted as soon as her foretelling name was spoken. Sunkskaa filled the vacuous quiet with more sharp, shrill, pulsating cries. Their jubilance resounded knowing that Matoaka meant "Snow Feather" or "White Feather." This baby girl was special, sacred. Her name would interminably link her to the iconic and salvific Swan and to Sky Woman.

Reverently, the Bringer of Prophecy plucked a white swan's feather from the fringe of her dress. She held Matoaka in one arm and extended the feather high above her head for all to see. Slowly, deliberately, even theatrically, the Bringer of Prophecy brought the feather toward the babe's face. She kissed the soft, pure plume then gently wove it into the nest of equally soft, but dark, baby hair on Matoaka's tiny head. The contrast of pitch-colored hair and bright feather was stunning, breathtaking. Its display could be seen from any seat in the quioccosan.

Matoaka released an enormous cry. As the Bringer of Prophecy handed the wailing baby back to her mother, sunk and sunksquaa broke into a vigorous song and dance. No one heard or noticed when the Bringer of Prophecy whispered into Matoaka's mother's ear her belief, "One day your daughter will bring peace and transformation to our people, the people of the *Powhatan*. She will follow the way of the *Apowa* (the Dream-Vision). Be sure she is steadfast in her training, and she will do unfathomable things."

By the time she was twelve, Matoaka had a love-hate relationship with her name. The name was the reason a band of children followed her everywhere she went, the reason warriors stopped sharpening their arrows to stare at her, the reason other girls in the village looked at her with eyes turquoise with jealousy. The name gave Matoaka the privilege of wearing white feathers in her hair; and usually made her feel like holding her chest high, doing cartwheels, skipping about the tribal town . . . but the name set her apart from the other girls.

The name solicited rigorous, sometimes torturous tutoring in the ways of the Beloved Woman. While the other girls in the village ran about fields learning to plant pumpkin, squash, and beans; hanging out with their mothers, gossiping, learning the art of tanning hides, nursing babies, and stringing shells, pearls, and sea shells . . . Matoaka's days were spent with *Weroansqua* (a priestly leader).

Weroansqua with her angular nose, stringy hair, and pock-marked face, was not physically beautiful like Matoaka. What she lacked in externalities, she made up for in soulful beauty, though. Her alluring wisdom and deeply intuitive nature made her the most powerful and desirable woman in the tribe. Often, Matoaka resented Weroansqua's ever-presence during Beloved Woman Discipleship. But, her earth-shaking insights into dreams and life (and even adolescence) made Weroansqua's constant presence endurable, even desirable, somehow.

Day after day, in ever-changing seasons and unpredictable weather, Matoaka and Weroansqua walked through the forest listening to the wind, trying to discover life-truths in the natural world, interpreting their dreams. As they walked together, Weroansqua's line of questioning was always the same: *What do you see? What do you hear? What do you feel? What is your dream-speak today? What are the colors of your dream-words? How is apowa dancing and singing and resting in you?*

Most of the training was more miserable than magnificent. The worst part had to be the fasting. At the beginning of every fast, Weroansqua would inevitably say, "You must be empty enough to have space for *apowa* (dream-vision)."

Mere hours into the fast, usually as the sun found its highest place in the sky, Matoaka would inevitably beg, "I'm starving. Please, just one piece of dried venison to keep me from fainting."

Weroansqua, refusing to waste words, merely shook her head.

Matoaka continued, "If I eat, I can concentrate better on my visions."

"No, child," the priestess would finally give up words while sitting still as a stone under a tree, listening for her own apowa. "You must follow the ways of *midéwewin* (spiritual discipline). You must bring a strong, weaned body and spirit to your calling as Beloved Woman. You must prepare and be ready for the day of Big Apowa, your life-dream."

The Big Apowa loomed large and monstrous before Matoaka. She worried that it would be as worthless as the dreams she'd already dreamed. The dreams Weroansqua had her etch into tanned deerskin. Dreams of chipmunks that Weroansqua said meant intelligence and resourcefulness. Dreams of rabbits jumping about that Weroansqua said meant mischief, shrewdness, creativity, a wild sense of humor. Matoaka dreamt of rabbits often. After years of deerskin journaling, dozens of her hides were covered with the furry, strong-legged, floppy-eared mammals. This made her teacher knowingly laugh.

When three wanton boys Matoaka's age noticed the drawings; they started calling the Beloved Woman-in-training a numinous nickname: *Pocahontas* (which meant playful, willful, mischievous and quick-witted like a bunny). The troublemakers tried to taunt Matoaka with the name. She rather liked it, though, and over time the appellation stuck.

Weroansqua was the only one in the village who refused to call the girl Pocahontas. For her purposes, the title given by the Bringer of Prophecy was the only appropriate name. By her lineage and bloodline, Pocahontas was Matoaka, and by Weroansqua's making, the girl hoped she might possibly—one day—become a Beloved Woman. In the deepest corner of her spirit, though, she felt more like a *Pocahontas*, than a *Matoaka*. And, she worried, "What if my Big Apowa is more about bunnies than about spirit?"

One winter day Pocahontas and Weroansqua practiced sacred dances for twelve hours in footprints the teacher had made in the snow. Rubbing her nearly frostbitten toes, Pocahontas said, "Feathers look so light when they're floating on the wind. Why do they feel so heavy in my hair?"

"It is a mystery, Matoaka," replied Weroansqua studying a snowflake crystal that had landed at the tip of Pocahontas's long braid.

"I don't think I'll ever be a Beloved Woman," the girl said breathlessly and crying.

Weroansqua lifted her gaze from the snowflake. Gently, she unbraided Pocahontas's hair. Then, carefully, she plucked five snow-white feathers from the girl's smooth, lacquer hair and held them in her fist.

Pocahontas continued to cry, "I don't think I'll ever be a Beloved Woman. I don't think I'll ever be a Beloved Woman. I don't think I'll ever be a Beloved Woman. I don't think I'll . . ."

Lifting her hands high in the air, Weroansqua opened her fist and released the feathers into a gust of winter wind, "Don't worry, Pocahontas, you already *are* a Beloved Woman."

It was just before spring equinox, time for twelve-year-old Pocahontas to receive her Big Apowa: the dream that would bring meaning, purpose, a life-mission or map . . . the dream that would set into course her chief responsibility and power. The power to spare the life of anyone—leader, warrior, or trespasser—accused of a crime and threatened by the death penalty. The power to make an irrevocable, undeniable decision of mercy that would absolutely override the power and authority of any man or woman, including the chief.

At dawn on the day of the dream, Pocahontas watched slants of sun squeeze their way between bark, animal skins, and the poles of her longhouse. The light, now dancing in dusty air, spun along with a panoply of emotions spinning within: fear, worry, eager anticipation, excitement, an overwhelming desire to stay under the warm hides that made up the bed. If she hadn't had to go to relieve herself, Pocahontas might've stayed in bed all day.

As Pocahontas emerged from behind an enormous oak, cold air wrapped around the girl like a heavy, unwelcome cloak. As Pocahontas walked back to the longhouse, she remembered the bedtime ritual of the night before. Weroansqua had been there. Just as she had so many times before, Pocahontas expected her mentor to tightly rebraid hair with white feathers, place shells, pearls, and other adornments around her neck, preparing for a sacred encounter.

Unexpectedly, Weroansqua moved with the quickness and tenacity of a grizzly bear, ripping the braids from Pocahontas' hair. Seemingly in a fit of madness, the sage woman vigorously rubbed Pocahontas's tresses into a snarled nest of black. The girl winced and drew her body back into a tight ball. Reaching toward the earthen longhouse floor, Weroansqua grabbed a handful of dirt. And reaching into the ball that was Pocahontas, found her face, grabbed it at the chin, and began smearing dirt all over cheeks, nose, forehead.

"What are you doing?" asked the girl, trying to resist the brutality by grabbing her mentor's forearms and pushing offending hands away.

"I am preparing you for your Big Apowa. When you wake in morning, you will look like *Nikomis* (the Woman Who Fell from the Sky): covered in earth, broken from your fall. In need and hopelessness, you'll be ready to meet the *manito* (spiritual guide, divine power). You, like *Nikomis*, will fall to a place where a new creation will be born from you. Big Apowa will come soon. I want you to be ready.

All of this seemed strange to Pocahontas. She wanted to resist it, rebel against it; in a way, though, being covered in dirt and ratting her hair was just what she desired. It inspired Pocahontas to scream and flail her tongue. But, she was too weak after the seemingly interminable and depleting five-day fast that had brought her to this moment. Pocahontas dropped her arms, let Weroansqua finish the dirty work and, exhausted, fell into a dreamless sleep. While she slept Weroansqua painted black temporary tattoos on the girl's chest, face, and hands: dots, dashes, geometric designs, zigzags, and hundreds of tiny, long-eared surprises.

As dawn illuminated the land in glowing orange, the Powhatan River moved with water and life. Trout and bass leapt out of the green waters to take a peek at the tall rustling grasses of the riverbank. Birds sang pentatonic melodies adorning the morning like beads on buckskin dresses. Pocahontas knew her sojourn to the *hobbomak* natural altar arrangement of rocks would be long and arduous. She didn't know how she'd do it without Weroansqua.

The voice of her teacher intruded her mind, cajoling and comforting, "Remember, journey must begin with a dance." Pocahontas didn't want to dance. Every sinew and bone in her body felt tired and weak from the fast and resentful toward all her dream-crazed responsibilities. She began moving her moccasins, anyway—slowly at first —in the patterned footwork she'd practiced hundreds of times. Forward, back, side, side. Stamp. Stamp. Turn and stamp. Forward, back, side, side. Stamp. Stamp. Turn and stamp.

Halfway through the sacred dance, Pocahontas still carried resentment on her shoulders like a bundle of wood. The rhythm and movement of the dance was hypnotic and helpful, though; it offered to carry the load. Pocahontas wasn't ready to yield the weight. With it she moved. Forward, back, side, side. Stamp. Stamp. Turn and stamp. The dance began to carry her. Heavy resentment, buoyed as small sparks of joy began to float into the dance, zipping a circuitous path within the girl. It inspired Pocahontas to swing her arms, raise them over her head. She began to laugh and to dance, *really* dance in a completely uninhibited way. The load fell off her back. She was readied for a Day of Big Dreaming.

Pocahontas took her first few steps out of the dance, and into the Great Field. Vernal grass was ankle high. It tickled, cold and damp. It was warmer than the ground beneath the forest canopy awaiting her, so Pocahontas took her time in the field. She looked at sky, numbered her steps, sallied along humming tunes her mother had sung to her as a baby.

In midmorning, the forest was dark and impenetrable to sun, except at its very edges. Entering the woods would feel the same way as getting out of bed had. She knew she'd have to brace herself, take a deep breath and just do it. Thankfully, the first few steps in weren't as bad as the Pocahontas imagined they'd be. Sun filtered in through forest-edge branches where the canopy was sparse. Pocahontas noticed a tree stump.

For a moment, she sat there, looking at the trees, the sky, then down at her hands. Pocahontas smiled when she caught a glimpse of Weroansqua's telling tattooed art: rabbits, hundreds of them, wily and wild-legged all over her hands, wrists, and arms. She enjoyed the artwork for a moment, then knew it was time to pass through the coldest part of the forest.

On the other side, Pocahontas removed her moccasins and crossed a familiar shallow stream. The water was crystal and as cold as cold could be. She bent down, cupped her hands and took countless insatiable drinks. She steadied herself across the stream with arms wide and wise choices between flat stepping stones protruding from frigid water.

In the near distance, she could see her hobbomak. The rock formation was megalithic and white with sun. She imagined how warm the rocks would feel when she sat on them, laid on them to take a well-earned nap. As Pocahontas rubbed silt off the soles of her feet and slipped back into her moccasins, she felt tempted to worry about the interminable duration (possibly days, even weeks) of her stay at the hobbomak. Instead, she ran toward the stone altar hoping to warm her bones and wishing the manito, Great Spirit, would come quickly.

Weroansqua came to the hobbomak every twelve hours. This was her fourth visit. Pocahontas, exhausted from sleeping on stones, nutritionally deprived, and spiritually discouraged, could barely respond to her teacher's presence.

"Drink this water, girl," Weroansqua begged a nearly incoherent Pocahontas.

"Jerky. Please . . . I need some . . . meat," the girl, could hardly speak. "I want to . . . go . . . home. Please . . . bring me . . . home. I want to be with . . . my . . . mother." Water dribbled out of the corners of her mouth as Weroansqua tried to pour a ladle of it past parched lips.

"You must stay and listen and wait," Weroansqua's voice was determined, underlined with a wisdom that comes from age and years of spiritual discipline. "Manito will visit. I feel the Big Apowa will come upon you soon. Be patient." And with that, the old woman crossed the stream and disappeared into the woods in a phantasmagorical flurry.

Pocahontas needed her mentor to stay. If she'd had the energy, she'd have asked Weroansqua to sleep at the hobbomak for at least one night. She wondered if her fear of the dark had kep*t* manito away. A shiver raced down her spine as she remembered the previous fitful night. A band of wolves had been particularly active and snarling. Every night Pocahontas could hear them rustling in the bushes behind her rocky resting place as they practiced clichéd howlings at the moon. Last night she heard them hunt down and kill a poor creature that cried and squeaked like a baby during the mauling, the carnivorous feasting. *The victim sounded like a rabbit*, she thought. Haplessly, she looked at her wrist, banded with leaping rabbits, and began to weep.

Now the noon sun was bright and luminous. It dried Pocahontas's tears into brown streaks on dirty cheeks. A red bird perching on a nearby branch caught the girl's eye. His song was intoxicating. Too tired to sit and watch him, she rested her head on the hobbomak rock, held her eyes half-open and listened to his metallic sounding melody: *whoit, whoit, whoit, what-cheer, what-cheer . . . wheet, wheet, wheet, wheet . . .* for what seemed like hours. The music entranced her. Somehow it lulled Pocahontas into a lucid dream.

The dream was like no other that she'd ever had. The colors were more vivid than the colors of the earth, the sounds more dramatic. Even the scents were intensified. The first smell she noticed was smoke. *Fire! Fire! There's a fire.* In the dream-vision, she ran about her land searching for fire. The fire wasn't in her village or the forest or field. She raced toward the river shore where she and Weroansqua sometimes collected valuable and rare shells. Her feet in sand, the scent of smoke intensified. Pocahontas looked north and south and still she could see no fire.

When she turned her gaze toward the ocean, there they were: three white, billowy tufts of smoke blowing in the breeze. *Where is the fire that makes this smoke?* she wondered. *And how can water burn?* The three white billows floated just above the waves and were rapidly nearing. As they approached, the ominous odor intensified. Now it was coming from the sea and from the village behind her. Screams of mothers and children floated ghoulishly in the air. The animals that had followed Pocahontas disappeared deep into the deepest part of forest. Pocahontas knew intuitively that her village was burning. Her people were dying. But there was nothing she could do; her feet were stuck in the sand. Not able to move, she stood on shore mesmerized by the billows.

As they got closer to land, Pocahontas noticed large — really enormous — canoes were attached to the billowy clouds. The canoes brought with them loud voices of men speaking in a strange and foreign tongue. The words were confusing, confounding, cryptic. One of the voices rose to the top of the din. Like a rope of words, the voice wrapped itself around one of the men, lifted him out of the big canoe and dropped him on shore at Pocahontas's feet. The man had skin of the palest shade, almost the color of a pearl. The sight of the whitened face covered with hair caused Pocahontas to shrink back with fear.

He tried to speak but the rope of words and ideas was wrapped so greedily around him that he seemed to have difficulty breathing. Pocahontas leaned down to unbind the stranger. As she did he began to choke. His eyes were frantic as if searching for air. And strangely, she noticed, the eyes were blue in color. Pocahontas wanted to stare, study, figure out how eyes could be the color of sky. She knew, though, that no time could be wasted. Quickly opening his mouth, she saw a large golden coin lodged in the stranger's throat. It blocked the airway. Carefully, she reached in and pulled out the obstruction.

The man gasped, and in gratitude whispered, "*Da-waè*" (thank you).

Pocahontas felt as if she was falling down a tunnel. The man's face was getting smaller and smaller. She gripped the coin with all her strength as she plummeted. Suddenly, her body came to a halt and she felt a rock beneath her head: the hobbomak. Without realizing that she'd been given her Big Apowa, Pocahontas sat up and lifted her hand to better examine the coin she gripped in a sweaty palm.

Opening her fist she stared in disbelief at an empty palm. Confused and disoriented, she held out her hand the way her father did when he hoped for rain. Her palm remained as lonely as an empty teepee until a sweet, fresh wind began blowing, bringing with it a large, white swan's feather. As if cosmically choreographed, the feather lit in the exact center of Pocahontas's outstretched palm. As the feather landed, the wind rested. In that very moment, Pocahontas knew spirit had come.

The moon was full, so was Pocahantas's belly. Her mother welcomed the girl home with a table full of friends and a feast of favorites: venison stew, corn on the cob, bright orange squash, spring beans, and bowls of sweet red berries. Weroansqua dined with the family for the ceremonious meal in celebration of the Big Apowa. After every savory bite, Pocahontas willfully resisted spilling the details of her dream-vision. Her spirit ached to tell the teacher, her mother's friends, and the rest of the family — to ask how they thought the images fit into the riddle of her life.

The conversation at Pocahontas's welcome home banquet was difficult for the girl to follow. The food and her hunger distracted her normally attentive ears. Women's voices overlapped. The story — told antiphonally — was confusing and frenzied. After an hour of her best listening, considering the circumstances, Pocahontas tried to condense the story in her mind:

*Three large canoes (that the women called ships) had landed on the shore away from Werowocómoco when Pocahontas was away.* Pocahontas wondered if the ships had anything to do with the white, billowy tufts of smoke in her dream. *Men from the ships — men with skin the color of snow — were establishing a new village on the Powhatan River. They called it by a strange name, Jamestown.* The name reminded Pocahontas of the foreign words that made a rope and wrapped 'round the strange man.

Pocahontas listened to the last part of the tale. The storyteller, one of the oldest women in the house, laughed a nervous kind of laugh when she said, "One of the White Men has been taken captive by the Chickahominy. Chief Powhatan has him now. They feast in the Big House tomorrow."

A girl of about sixteen, sitting beside her mother, said, "His name is John Smith." Her tongue tripped on the unfamiliar consonants and vowels in the name. "When the moon is next full, at the Great Feast of Nikomis, the Woman Who Fell from the Sky, he will come to trial. I heard Powhatan plans to kill him!"

Pocahontas felt sick. The warm meal churned in her belly along with a burning temptation to tell the women her dream. She knew better of doing that before meeting with Weroansqua. Instead, and in a whisper resounding like a breeze, she said, "Maybe the Chief will decide to spare this one, this John Smith."

The moon was full again. January 8, 1608. The *Tsenacommacah* (the land belonging to the tribes of the Powhatan Alliance) was pregnant with anticipation for the Feast of Nikomis. Hundreds of leaders from the entire Powhatan Alliance camped on the outskirts of Werowocómoc, the land of Pocahontas's tribe. The men wore their finest headdresses. The women were adorned with crownlets of white clamshells signifying a time of rebirth.

Weroansqua braided tens of swans' down feathers into Pocahontas's ash-black hair. It was the first time since the Big Apowa that the teacher pulled long locks tight, inflicting pain on the girl's scalp. It was the first time Pocahontas did not complain. During this ceremonial ritual, affirming Pocahontas's sacred lineage by birth and training, the Beloved Woman felt as if she'd finally *become* the woman heralded by the feathers.

Pocahontas stood beside Weroansqua at the east opening of the tent, watching the procession. Chief Powhatan and his queen were the first to enter. He sat halfway down the north side of the hall on a large bench running the length of the quioccosan, Great House, temple. The queen sat directly across from him on a bench running along the south side of the Great House. As the couple breezed by Pocahontas, she caught a whiff of the power that used to intoxicate her. Today it smelled bland and inconsequential.

Priests, weroances, weroanskaas, sunks, and sunkaas entered next, moving in a measured, rhythmic dance step. Their ankles, adorned with turtle-shell rattles, sang a percussive song as they stepped in patterned movement. On the way to wide benches behind Powhatan, the men tossed pinches of tobacco into the fire as an honorary gift. The fire surged and sparked in gratitude. The women followed and sat on narrow benches in a higher, second tier of seating. Thirty groups of male warriors, representing each of the thirty tribes in the Powhatan Alliance, were the penultimate groups to file in. One of the last warriors to enter had the skin of a bird, with wings outstretched, perched on top of his head. From his waist hung the dried hand of one of his enemies.

All the men and women had heads and shoulders painted with red pigment they'd ground from *puccoon* root and mixed with bear grease. Pocahontas touched her red cheek. The oily cosmetic clung to her finger. She dotted it on the middle of one of the rabbit tattoos decorating her wrist. Noticing a young, antsy Beloved-Woman-in-training standing behind her, Pocahontas felt tempted to whisper that red was a sign of rebirth, hope, renewal, and love. She kept silent.

Now was the time for Weroansqua, and Pocahontas, the Beloved Women, and Beloved Women in training from the twenty-nine other tribes to enter. The girls flitted in like a flock of signets. Some of the Beloved Women were so young they couldn't help but giggle at the solemnity of the moment. Pocahontas grabbed one particularly giggly girl by the shoulder and squeezed hard enough to make her stop. Chief Powhatan shot deathly glances their way to immediately stifle the rest. If she had a chance, Pocahontas promised herself that she'd tell the girls about Powhatan. He was known for his strong leadership . . . by his followers and any tribe that attempted to assert itself and interfere with his rule. The results could be deadly. Now was not the time for stories.

Gourd rattles shook as the officiating priest—who wore a nest of stuffed snakeskins and weasels in his hair, their tails tied in a tangled topknot—sanctimoniously opened the feast with a blessing. Pocahontas felt charged with a surprisingly loving energy.

Powahatan nodded toward the east entrance and immediately the entire *quioccosan* (great house) was silenced as thirty guards escorted a prisoner toward the chief. It was difficult for Pocahontas to see the stranger, a pale man, as he walked in, surrounded by a small army of guards. Straining her head to see past the furious fire, she hoped to get a glimpse of his face, but she could not.

Chief Powhatan laid corn and sticks in a pattern around the fire, further obscuring the girl's view. Then, a great bowl of venison was presented to the prisoner: an offering of friendship. Though Pocahontas strained to see the stranger's face, it was still obscured by the flames. All she could see was one of his pale hands as it pushed away the bowl of food. She wasn't surprised when he rejected the meal.

Raising his arms, the chief summoned warriors to place two large flat rocks on the ground in front of the prisoner. One of the rocks was painted red; the other was black. Pocahontas remembered from her training that black and red juxtaposed meant metamorphosis. The rocks in place, two warriors dragged the man to Powhatan's feet and placed his head upon the flat stones. Pocahontas could finally see the face. She gasped loud enough for the chief to hear. *The face was the face from her dream. The blue eyes: those of the man whose life she saved in her Big Apowa.*

The chief ignored the outburst as two men wielding clubs moved toward the prisoner, weapons raised high above their heads. As the priest made a threatening gesture toward the captive, Pocahontas felt an unexpected, high, vibrating shriek emerge from her mouth. It was the tremolo of joy and welcome. It made Pocahontas blush with its complete incongruity in the moment. Regardless, she continued to shriek. And, suddenly, without realizing that her body was launching off of the bench, Pocahontas threw her own body over the dream-man and laid her head on top of his.

The gesture became frozen in time as if an almighty tableau. The only thing in the big house that moved was the fire. Pocahontas could not breathe until she heard a communal wail being released from all the people. It was their affirmation of her power as a Beloved Woman — their affirmation of a life spared, protected, saved.

Pocahontas began to sing, the man still beneath her, shaking. She sat up and looked into the man's eyes with compassion and newly born authority. A warrior who knew the words of the blue-eyed man approached and translated a shaky conversation.

The prisoner sat up too. He could hardly speak. "I am John Smith." His name was the name from her dream!

"I am Pocahontas," she said as she knelt beside him. "Your new name will be Capahowasick," she said, knowing that now that his life had been spared, John Smith would be adopted into her tribe. "I will be your teacher. I will teach you in the ways of our people."

The man did not understand. He looked at her with questions behind his eyes and weakness that only allowed him to say two more words, "Da-wa'e."

Pocahontas visited Jamestown and her new friend, John Smith, traveling on foot. She brought provisions that saved his troops from malnutrition and warned him of pending attacks. Weroansqua continued to school the now sixteen-year-old girl in the ways of the Beloved Woman. In turn, she schooled John Smith about listening to the wind and dreams and the cycles of the moon.

Around this time Smith got wounded and was shipped back to England for medical treatment. And Pocahontas came to live in Henricus, about fifty miles upriver from the Jamestown settlement. While living there for a year, the teen fell in love with one of the Englishmen there, John Rolfe. During that year, Pocahontas's love for John and his desire that she become a Christian (so they could wed) compelled her to study this man's beliefs. In her village, the Beloved Women had heard stories of the English forcing the People to convert. Her experience was completely different.

Pocahontas's tutors in the Christian faith, including Smith, engaged in a satisfactory exchange with her. The discipleship reminded Pocahontas a lot of her times with Weroansqua. But, the experience

CHAPTER 8

was even richer because the teaching was mutual. She taught the settlers how to be careful, quiet listeners . . . she took them deep into the forest and helped them pick nonpoisonous berries and mushrooms. They gave her new recipes for preparing the foods she provided, and educated her in the Bible. She told them how she met with the manito spirit on the hobbomac rock. They told her how they met with God in a small structure within the compound called a *church*. She took them to her hobbomac; they invited her to church and told Pocahontas about Peter, the rock on which the Christian church was built.

There was something about the church at Jamestown that reminded Pocahontas of the hobbomac. It was safe and warm and solid. When she sat beside John Smith listening to Bible readings — in English which she was beginning to understand — in a strange way she felt like she simultaneously belonged to her people and with this new foreign band. Her spirit was free and affirmed when she heard stories from the Bible. They seemed to complete ideas she'd learned in her Beloved Woman training.

In 1613 Pocahontas asked to be baptized. The day of her ceremony, women of Jamestown dressed the Native American in a huge, heavy skirt. Stiff, tapestry fabric covered her torso, arms, and neck. *The religion is much more comfortable than their clothes,* thought Pocahontas. The ritual garbs reminded her strangely of the night Weroansqua covered her in dirt.

Sitting beside John in their normal spot in the sanctuary, she tugged at her stiff collar and unbuttoned the first two buttons of the blouse exposing a beautiful purple and white wampum necklace given to her by her mother. In her braided hair was a white swan feather.

The pastor had his big, black Bible open toward the very end. "Stand for the reading of God's Word," he said in a distinguished and theatrical voice that filled the small structure. He cleared his throat and continued, "A reading from the Book of 1 John, chapter 3. 'For this is the message you have heard from the beginning, that we should love one another . . .'" John scooted closer to his fiancée. She could feel the warmth of his arm through the uncomfortable blouse. "'Not as Cain, who slew his brother . . . We know that we have passed out of death into life, because we love the brethren. He who does not love abides in death. Everyone who hates his brother is a murderer; and you know that no murderer has eternal life abiding in him . . .'"

Scenes of neighboring villages burning to the ground flashed through Pocahontas's mind. Fights between her native people and her new family: arrows, rifles, horses . . . raced loud and destructively within. She wondered why both of the peoples she loved couldn't love each other. The preacher spoke loudly with a perspicacious passion, "We know love by this, that we ought to lay down our lives for the brethren . . ." The preacher laid the big book down on the altar. Pocahontas knew this was when he'd start walking around, telling stories, "giving the sermon," as John called it.

"Brothers and Sisters, I'm here to tell you today that Jesus laid down His life for us . . ."

Pocahontas didn't hear another word of the sermon. With that short sentence she had an epiphany, an epiphany about Jesus. *Maybe the Beloved Woman is a type of Christ sort of,* she imagined. So excited, the words almost came aloud. Instead, Pocahontas quietly savored her connection. As she did, the Beloved Woman was taken back to the Feast of Nikomis, the day when she placed herself in jeopardy for John Smith. In her mind she relived every smell and sight and sound of the day. When she got to the part where she threw her tiny frame on the convicted man, the pastor took her arm and brought her to the baptismal. John walked to the altar with her. She leaned her head over the tub and a river of water cooled and wet her forehead and trickled into her braid.

The pastor orated, "I now baptize you in the name of the Father, the Son, and the Holy Spirit. From this day forward you shall be called Lady Rebecca." The entire congregation started clapping. The service ended. Dozens of congregants threw happy arms around Pocahontas, heartily congratulating her in English *and* her native tongue. She hugged them back.

With her face and hair still wet, she noticed Weroansqua at the front of the church, beside a picture of Jesus. He stood in a white robe, arms outstretched, slants of sun radiating behind Him. The wise woman opened her arms for Pocahontas in a mirroring of Jesus' gesture. Pocahontas went to her. As Weroansqua embraced Pocahontas, the

Beloved Woman noticed the hands of Jesus, scarred by the nails she'd heard about. Tucking a wet strand of hair behind her ear, Pocahontas leaned into the embrace and toward the painting. Her eyes followed one of the slants of light down Jesus' arm until it touched His open palm. Studying the scar, Pocahontas noticed — over the shoulder of her spiritual guide — that the jagged hole in Jesus' hand looked to her to be almost the shape of a swan feather.

## AFTER THE STORY

In April of 1614, with the approval of Chief Powhatan, Pocahontas — now Lady Rebecca — married English tobacco planter, John Rolfe. She had one child with him, whom they named Thomas. In 1616 she was the toast of England, summering in the country at Lyon House on banks of Thames, taking long walks, going to picnics, games, meeting the queen, dancing. On a ship heading for her indigenous home in 1617, Pocahontas got gravely ill and was hurried to Gravesend, a small English port, where she died. Pocahontas was buried on March 21, 1617 (at the age of 21). Her son left with John Rolfe's brother in England.

Her work as an ambassador, priestess, and Beloved Woman will never be forgotten. Some consider Pocahontas to be the mother of the new world, the female counterpart to George Washington. She walked the way of love. During a time of conflict, she brought peace. During a time of division, she united. During a time of narrowmindedness, she connected the sacred to the everyday. She was involved in a world of change because it was the role and responsibility of a Beloved Woman to do so, and Pocahontas became a Beloved Woman of God in the truest sense.

## PONDERINGS FOR THE HEART:
### *Reflecting on God's Love*

Pocahontas held a sacred role in the early development of the United States. She was a Beloved Woman, searching for love, listening to dreams, bridging the gap between two very different people groups, hoping for peace. Among the several roles she filled, the primary one may have been her role as Beloved Woman. Though her life was wrought with trials and determination, she left a legacy for all women who can be creative agents of healing, redemption. She made a way for experiencing the love of God within the context of unique multicultural, social, historical, and familial surroundings.

> *Were there two sides to Pocahontas? Did she have a fourth dimension?*
> — ERNEST HEMINGWAY

1. At one point in her training, Pocahontas doubted her identity as a Beloved Woman. Have you ever doubted your Christian identity as a Beloved Bride of Christ, one chosen and holy and pure in God's sight? Is it difficult or easy for you to see yourself as beloved? Do you feel that you have merely been chosen to be a woman of faith because of heritage, life circumstances? Take some time to journal about this.

2. Is there anyone (or has there been anyone) who has introduced you to spiritual disciplines like prayer and fasting and solitude? If so, what did you learn from this person? Write down this person's name. Then, make a list identifying what she has taught you. Would you ever consider being a spiritual mentor for another woman? How do you imagine this playing out in your life? Daydream or write about your answer.

3. The gift of the Beloved Woman is her life dream. Do you have a God-given dream or vision for your life? Take a moment to consider God's dream for you. This could be a calling, a divine hope, a word of direction from Christ. It could be long-term or meant for this season alone. It could be a sentence, a paragraph, or a word. Listen for it. And, consider taking the time to write it down.

# HEARTBEATS:
## Acting on God's Love

1.  The theme of redemption runs through the story of Pocahontas. In a salvific move, she covered John Smith, sparing him. On the day of her baptism, Pocahontas realized that she was a Christlike figure. Do you feel that you've ever been asked to "cover" someone else, to "save" them or an aspect of their life? How have, or could, you be a redemptive force in your world? Perhaps the answers to these questions could be grand or ordinary: as simple as caring for the child of one of your friends, who has a terminally ill spouse, bringing a meal to someone who has just had surgery, or giving time to serve at a food pantry or soup kitchen.

2.  White swans' feathers play an important role in Pocahontas's story. They are the indication that she's a Beloved Woman. It took the girl almost the entire story before she felt comfortable wearing feathers in her hair. Whether you feel like it or not, you're beloved too. Consider doing something to your external appearance to remind yourself of this: perhaps don a special piece of jewelry, a hat, or a certain color that represents love to you. If you're feeling a little crazy, braid a white feather in your hair for the day.

3.  Have you experienced spiritual disciplines that have helped you hear God's voice? Lectio divina? Journaling? Meditative prayer? Scripture reading? Daily devotions? Centering prayer? Recording your dreams? Consider what works for you. Try to make time in your week this week to pursue and enjoy that practice.

4.  Pocahontas has numerous names in her life: Beloved Woman, Matoaka, Pocahontas, Lady Rebecca Rolfe. Because our names can bear our spiritual, social, familial, and cultural identity, take a moment to complete the following poem schema as a way of considering aspects of your name and identity. If you're getting serious in the

writing, be playful; if you're feeling playful, consider a more sobering thought. Be free in the writing, have fun:

I AM

Yesterday, my name was _____ ;

Today is _____ .

Tomorrow my name will be _____ .

My spouse, friend, boss, or child thinks my name is

_____ and

God, whose name is Love, calls me _____ .

5. God talked to Joseph and Mary and many others through their dreams. He has revealed His Word to us through Christ, and a basis for our lives in the Scriptures. Consider recording your dreams for a day, week, month, or longer. Spend times in the Scriptures. Use the following questions to help you hear God's voice: *What themes, imagery, reoccurring ideas, or characters or symbols are consistently showing up in my dreams and times of devotion? What might God be saying to me?*

6. Pocahontas fasted. Fasting is not easy. But, it has the potential of creating space within us for a greater connection with God's love. Consider making a fast (please do your research and check with your doctor before you begin).

> *She has been called the First Lady of America, a Daughter of Eve, a Child of the Forest, a Madonna Figure, the Nonparallel of Virginia, the Mother of Us All, and the Great Earth Mother of the Americas.*
>
> — CHARLES R. LARSON

# CHAPTER 9

## Harriet Gives a Grace Out of Nothing

### THE FACTS

NAME: Araminta Ross (at birth), Araminta Tubman (when married to John Tubman around 1844), Harriet Tubman (once freed from slavery), Mrs. Harriet Davis (when married to Nelson Davis in 1869).

DATE OF BIRTH: c. 1820 (No written record of Harriet Tubman's birth exists.)

DATE OF DEATH: March 10, 1913

OTHERWISE KNOWN AS: Minty, the Moses of Her People, General Tubman

SUMMARY: Araminta Ross was born into slavery at the turn of the nineteenth century. According to family lore, she was one of 11 children. Through prayer and a dose of sass, Araminta survived a horrific childhood and adolescence enslaved on the Brodess plantation near Bucktown, Maryland. Her resourcefulness and spunk preserved her life and unavoidably brought her freedom in the fall of 1849 when she made her escape from slavery. With a new name — Harriet Tubman — and the sweet taste of freedom on her lips this paragon in the abolition movement became a conductor on the Underground Railroad.

ഏ TRIVIA: A plethora of angry plantation owners, most assuming that the so-called Moses was a man, were outraged to discover the contrary. They placed a $100 to $1,000 dollar reward on Harriet's head for aiding and abetting runaway slaves (some reported it was as much as $40,000). Despite swarms of bounty hunters on the Liberty Lines and thanks to numerous disguises, cunning, and subterfuge, Harriet Tubman was never recognized or detained.

ഏ NOTABLE: In April 1897 Queen Victoria sent Harriet a Diamond Jubilee medal and a letter inviting her to England. Minty never made the trip. It is said, though, that despite being illiterate Harriet unfolded and stared at the letter so often it became "as thin as a shadow."

ഏ QUOTABLE: When Araminta crossed into Pennsylvania, she felt she was reborn and renamed herself Harriet, and said

> *"I looked at my hands to see if I was the same person now that I was free. There was such a glory over everything: the sun came like gold through the trees, and over the fields, and I felt like I was in heaven."*
>
> — HARRIET TUBMAN (from M. W. Taylor's
> *Harriet Tubman: Antislavery Activist*)

---

A MAXIM OF THE STORY: *Harriet Tubman was neglected and abused, bereft of wages, material comforts, and security. She had nothing yet would grow up to be legendary conductor on the Underground Railroad. Though she was financially impoverished, out of her bereftness, she created gifts of grace for others with a gracious and splendorous tenacity, in partnership with her God who creates out of nothing, as He did at Creation.*

---

The apples falling at Brodess plantation of Maryland were particularly red and round. Seven-year-old Araminta Ross salivated as she picked and polished one red orb after another, placing each in baskets for the Big House. It was against Master Brodess's rules for a slave to eat a scant bite at harvest. Somehow these draconian boundaries made the fruit appear even more succulent to Minty. They enticed, even tempted her. Hanging from slender, brown stems, the apples seemed to taunt, *Just take one little bite. No one will ever know. Do it* now . . . *while the overseer isn't looking!* Day after day she wondered what it'd taste like to crunch a crisp chunk of flesh 'tween her teeth, or feel fresh sweet juices rolling down her chin.

Hand shaking, the young girl reached for a ripe beauty on a branch inches above her head. At the precise moment the apple snapped free from the tree, a flock of small, brown birds soared from the field into the sky. Araminta palmed the apple, redirecting her focus on the birds. They looked like choreographed confetti, and seemed to want Minty to know how much better flight was than pecking about the grass.

Her eyes dropped from the birds back to the apple, then up and down her secluded row of trees. *The Overseer must be at the other end of the orchard,* she thought. Slowly, with much anticipation and salivation, Araminta raised the shiny red beauty to her lips. Just as she opened her mouth ready to bite, an indomitable itch on her right shoulder blade detracted her. *Confound this burlap mess of a dress,* she whispered under her breath while fiercely scratching. Until just recently she had not had to wear anything, as she was only a child.

Indian summer made the clothing particularly insufferable. The uniform wasn't going to stop Minty from enjoying the sweet fruit of her labor, though. Itch slaked, she once more scanned the red and green row. No overseer.

The apple found its way to her mouth. Then, "*Crunch!*" A moment of pure bliss! Her work seemed momentarily lighter, a ray of extraordinary warm kissed Araminta's ordinary day.

Then, suddenly, as if out of air he appeared. Before a drop of rewarding juice could near the corner of Minty's mouth, the overseer grabbed her. "What do you think you're doin'?"

In a pall of anger, he threw the young girl to the ground. Immediately she curled into the fetal position, hoping, praying that the wretched uniform would create some kind of buffering armor against the whip. It did not. Instead it yielded, easily splaying beneath cutting blows of the overseer's whip; embedding itself deeply into dozens of lacerations that erupted in red lines all over Minty's vulnerable flesh.

She tried to move but the eyelids on her closed eyes refused to budge. The sound of the overseer cursing, his feet pounding earth as he walked away reverberated an eerie echo in Minty's ringing ears. She lay on the ground for what felt like an eternity. Then, as clear, promising, and warm as an orchard breeze, Araminta heard from within herself, a promising voice, *One day you will have all the apples you would ever want to eat.*

Minty believed the voice belonged to God. Even in her disoriented state, she trusted the promise. It flooded her broken body with bravery and impassioned resolve. It summoned a fleck of strength just big enough to help open her eyes. As they cracked, all she could see was her apple on the ground. One bite out of it, covered in dirt and bees. Motivating anger mingling with belief, and Araminta grunted to stand. In her heart she vowed, *When I get those apples . . . I'm going to eat my fill . . . and have so many left I'll have to give them away.*

That night a slashed and sore Araminta Ross was on call in the nursery at the Big House. Despite the afternoon's whipping, it was still Minty's job to keep Miss Susan's six-month-old from crying and awaking his mother. At two hours past midnight, the baby boy began to whimper. In fear of another lashing, the young slave picked up the baby and began pacing the cold, damp hall outside the nursery. Each time she passed the doorway, she counted. "One, two . . . fifty-three . . . eighty-eight . . . one hundred eleven."

As she paced with Miss Susan's babe in her arms, Minty's eyes seemed as heavy as the cherubic bundle. Her head nodded, begging for sleep. A vision of Miss Susan flashed into Araminta's sleep-deprived mind, bolting her into a stomach-sick wakefulness. The sight added to Minty's existing nausea: cloaked beneath a mountain of quilts, one glowing white arm hung over the edge of the bed. In the hand, the ubiquitous brown leather whip, held in a white-knuckled nocturnal grip.

Miss Susan's baby wriggled in Minty's arms. He rubbed his eyes. Minty tried bouncing him, patting him, soothing him by pacing the hall a few more times. He arched his back, red-cheeked and ready to wail. The apple promise that had fortified Minty mere hours ago seemed like a distant delusion. In this moment, she needed real, practical help with skin on.

With passion and resolve born of desperation, she prayed, *Lord, I'm asking you . . . please help this baby sleep. You know what's gonna happen to me if Miss Susan hears even one peep. I'll be whipped again, God. So please, help me. Help me, Jesus! Hold me while I hold this baby. I'm asking You again . . . beggin' You, please make this baby sleep!*

"Waaaaaaaaaah! Waaaaaah! Waaaaaaah!" Angry steps. Another lashing. Gashes, just beginning to coagulate, burst open in ferocious stinging reminders of her emptiness.

In 1844, Araminta Ross, at age nineteen, married freed black man John Tubman. With her parents, Harriet (nicknamed Rit) and Benjamin along with ten brothers and sisters watching, Minty and John "jumped the broom." With the broom handle skimming a mere inch above the floor, the bride and groom held hands and jumped backwards over it. The handle was raised and they jumped again. On the third jump, Minty let go of John's hand, feeling inspired by a deeply competitive nature.

Four jumps later, John was breaking a sweat and his new bride just grinned and waved hands at the sky, daring the broom to be elevated more. On the eighth backward jump, John stumbled. Minty smiled a broad, warm smile, hugged her man, and whispered in his ear, "You know what this means, J. T. For the rest of our lives you're going to have to heed my wishes!" As the family cheered, Araminta and John Tubman shared a long, playful kiss that faded into the deepest, happiest kind of laughter.

Laughter soon surrendered to "weeping time" when Master Brodess sold Araminta Tubman's sisters, Linah and Soph, to a Georgia trader. Minty would never forget the tormented looks on her siblings' faces. Their countenances were hollow, tragic, and despairing and her mind's eye captured their howling screams. Minty's life, all at once, emptied of two of her most important relationship, of sisterhood itself. As they were dragged away from Mama Rit, soon to disappear into the Deep South, Minty remembered a story her mother had told mere days earlier.

The entire family sat beneath a twisty ancient oak at the corner of the plantation. Rit spoke with a spellbinding kind of sagaciousness. She leaned forward simultaneously whispering and warning her brood of ills that lurked around every corner if you were a slave. She shook a curved index finger at each of her progeny, "I heard through the grapevine that Caroline, from the plantation up the road, was forced to the auction block with her husband and three children. A Georgia trader took a liking to Caroline and bought her on the spot."

Wind blew through deciduous branches. Minty leaned closer to John, nestling her head where it fit perfectly: in the warm crook right between his strong shoulder and neck. Rit continued, "Caroline looked the devil trader square in the eye. 'Have you bought my husband?' she asked. The devil shook his head, no. Stepping off the block and approaching the man, Caroline planted her feet squarely on the ground and asked another question, 'Have you bought my children?'

"The answer, again, was no. Without blinking an eye, Caroline went into the courtyard, grabbed an axe, and chopped off her left hand."

Araminta gasped loudly, air expanding her chest. Several of the children stared at the ground. A few of the girls sniffed back tears. Benjamin, Minty's father, exhaled audibly then took Rit's hand in his, squeezing her fingers together, then bringing them toward his mouth to kiss. "Lord have mercy, Mother!"

Rit continued, "Caroline walked back to her purchaser as if nothing had happened and told him to go 'head and take her. One look at the bloody wrist made the man vomit. He left town in a whirlwind, and Caroline got to stay with her kin."

The story flashed and faded as quickly as the men dragged Soph and Linah from the plantation. For a moment, Araminta worried that Rit would find an axe and dismember herself in an act of desperation. Instead, the matriarch sank into a corner, diminishing into a ball of weeping. She sobbed deeply and uncontrollably at this loss almost worse than death. Araminta wrapped a quilt around her mother trying to bring a measure of comfort. In her soul, she knew there wouldn't be any. There'd be no closure, funeral, or solace either; just an empty, bellyaching, hungry, chronic kind of mourning.

With the sisters gone forever, Araminta and John Tubman felt mounting pressures to produce a child. Most days the prospect of grandbabies was the only thing that put even a scant glimmer into Rit's eyes. Though the couple feared bringing a baby (who could be taken from them at any moment) into the world, they also took stock in the redemptive power of new life, in the joys birth and babies bring even in the eye of loss.

Near the end of every month, Araminta experienced promising symptoms: sensitive breasts, swollen abdomen, irritability. Hope rose to the top of her heart like cream in a pail. Then the red reason for her symptoms would plummet Minty into frustration. And the hope-frustration-emptiness cycle would roll on.

This cycle continued for five years. During her infertile season, Araminta's hope morphed into anger. She began having visions and nightmares of hoofbeats and women's screams, of horsemen riding in to kidnap slaves. At first the newlywed blamed the spells on the head injury she'd sustained as an adolescent. She was thirteen years old when a two-pound weight struck her in the head, during a scuffle between a field hand and an overseer.

Minty remembered throwing her body between the two men. Then watching when — as if in slow motion — the overseer picked up the weight and threw it at the male slave. When the ad hoc missile missed its target, Minty instinctively ducked. That's when searing pain bloomed above her left eye; she heard her skull crack and the world went black. The injury was severe, causing the young girl to slip into a six-week coma and suffer narcoleptic episodes for the rest of her life.

During Araminta's woundedness, Rit sat by her daughter's sickbed, praying and recounting every Bible story she could. One that returned to Araminta's memory — like the coda at the end of a symphony — was Moses' exodus from Egypt as he led the enslaved Israelites to liberty. Indelible were images of God's man standing before Pharaoh demanding, "Let my people go!" Inspiring were tales of plagues and passages through a sea of red, a desert with manna, to a land of promise. The promise of emptiness filled in a land of plenty.

Unforgettable was God's vow to Moses that Rit, though illiterate, could quote verbatim,

> Because of my mighty hand [Pharaoh] will let them go; because of my mighty hand he will drive them out of his country. . . . I will free you from being slaves to them, and I will redeem you with an outstretched arm and with mighty acts of judgment. I will take you as my own people, and I will be your God. Then you will know that I am the LORD your God, who brought you out from under the yoke of the Egyptians. And I will bring you to the land I swore with uplifted hand to give to Abraham" (EXODUS 6:1, 6–8 NIV).

Day after day, in her bed of sickness, Araminta drank these words. They were the only thing that slaked her thirst for hope. After recovering and gaining enough strength to rise from the bed, Minty voraciously ate the words. She feasted on them, putting them to memory like her mother. While harvesting apples, rocking babies, hoisting barrels of flour, Minty ruminated on their promise. In extraordinary ways the words fortified her spirit. They became daily food: a piece of yeasty, leavened hope wrapped in the crust of promise.

Certain verses sustained Araminta during uncertain times. When Soph and Linah were sold, Araminta repeated, *Because of my mighty hand He will let them go.* Minty wondered if God would, one day, let her sisters go. She also wondered if, in a strangely symbolic way, Rit kept her hand (instead of hacking it off as Caroline did) because she thought she'd need it — like God — to be mighty and freeing for her family.

Later, when Minty executed a prayer vigil asking God to "either change or kill Master Brodess," and the tyrant died, she rejoiced in the words, *I will free you from being slaves, and I will redeem you with an outstretched arm and with mighty acts of judgment.* But, when Brodess's sons inherited and maintained the slave status of Minty's family, treating them worse than Brodess himself, the young slave realized she would *act* on God's promises in order to be a recipient of the hope they espoused. She was called to live out her freedom, walk it step by perilous and arduous step.

Inexorably missing her sisters, struggling with infertility, wearied from a life as human chattel, battling narcolepsy, harboring fear of being sold into the Deep South, Araminta was desperate and despairing. Regularly she spoke with her husband, John, about fleeing to the North. He was bound by all that was slavery; she was zealous to escape.

On a chilly September evening in 1849, Minty sat in the arms of an apple tree on the Brodess plantation, staring into the charcoal sky at the North Star. With unharnessed spiritual mettle born of anger, exhaustion, and hope, Minty recited aloud, *I will bring you to the land I swore to give you.* As the words echoed down a row of trees, she remembered every detail of Moses' adventures in Egypt and beyond. Story playing out in her mind, the outline of old, staff wielding, white-bearded Moses began to blur.

He was metamorphosing in Minty's mind. Slowly his stature shrank to about five feet. His skin, though burnished, darkened. His curly hair kinked. A scar formed on the left side of the brow. As Moses disappeared, a black-hued woman appeared. *Who is that woman?* Minty's conscience asked the midnight sky, though, in her heart, she already knew the answer.

A billowing voice coming from just south of the North Star replied, *It is you, my Beloved. Now go!*

In an anointed split second, the young slave from Maryland accepted her place of action. She was ready to go. Fear mingled with adrenaline that night. Araminta Tubman couldn't sleep. The next morning she'd set off to forge a way for herself and her fellow slaves to cross into a land of freedom, cold winters, and promise.

The North Star and moon shone particularly bright on the evening of Minty's departure. And, by some spectacular grace, everyone on the Brodess plantation — including John Tubman — slept soundly. With two torn slips of paper held tightly in her hand, a shaking Araminta Tubman stared at her sleeping husband, memorizing the lines on his face by moonlight. She longed to tell him her plan, heartily hug and kiss him, languish over long good-byes. (Minty forfeited official good-byes for fear that knowledge of her plan of escape would earn her family chastisement: whippings or worse, death by gallows.)

As careful and tender as a falling leaf, Minty kissed her husband's forehead, then gingerly unfolded the scraps of paper. Each bore a name and directions to a house on the Liberty Lines. *Liberty Lines,* a kind free woman told Araminta, *were pathways on the Underground Railroad where fugitives are escorted north.* Minty was baffled and invigorated by the verbal subterfuge surrounding the Underground Railroad. According to the woman there were *stationmasters, depots* or *safe houses, conductors,* even *cargo* (secret code for fugitives). With gratitude for the information, Araminta gave the woman a prized quilt. With a soft, warm, vein-laced old hand the woman pressed the scraps of paper into Minty's palm. *"These are your tickets," the woman said, "Don't lose 'em."* Minty looked at the names and directions on the scraps. They appeared as meaningless squiggles and lines to her.

The slave's perplexed look prompted the woman to assure one more thing. "It doesn't matter that you can't read the tickets, dear. You'll recognize friendly folk along the lines. Show 'em what I've written, and they'll help you. Godspeed!"

Araminta's first steps outside Brodess plantation boundaries were slow and tentative tiptoes. Cool, wet grass shocked and tickled her ankles. For a short stretch she walked backward watching, even hoping, to get one last glimpse of her family. She scanned the familiar acres, worried that an overseer might spy her in the nighttime shadows. She whispered, "Good-bye, John; good-bye, family; . . . good-bye, apple orchard." And she watched her visible breath in cold air disappear like smoke. The farther Minty got from home, the more her pace accelerated, the less she looked back.

Her hastening heartbeat kept time. Kaaaaaaaaaaaaah. Thuuuuu-uuuunk. Kaaaah-thuuunk. Kaah-thunk, ka-thunk, kathunk, kathunk-kathunk-kathunk-kathunk! Beating coursed through Minty's arms and legs, pulsated in her ears. The vociferousness of the poundings surprised her. At a forest's edge Araminta let loose, coursing full-speed, pushing her faculties to their limits. Twigs snapped beneath her feet, sapling tree branches scraped her face and chest. With nostrils flared, head back, mouth open begging for oxygen Minty ran. She ran until a stitch in her side demanded that she lay her body down in the midnight purple grass. Sprawled beneath the sky, chest heaving, eyes shut, Araminta had a vision:

She was flying over towns and fields and rivers and mountains, looking down on them like a bird. After flying for quite a distance, she reached a megalithic brick fence. She tried to fly over it, but could not. Sinking down, strength spent, three ladies (all dressed in white) appeared. They stretched out their arms toward Minty and pulled her over.

New beginnings are filled with sensory experiences: sights, aromas, melodies, tastes, sensations. Because Araminta walked over ten miles a day for three weeks, pain from blisters and abrasions marked Araminta's new beginning. The smell of *asafetida* did too. To elude the dogs of bounty hunters, Minty rubbed resin-like gum from foul-smelling asafetida herb on the bottoms of her feet. The resin stunk like rotten onions or fennel. With each step in the forest or along the Choptank River, she inhaled the wretched odor. For miles at a time Minty repeated the herb's common name, devil's dung, devil's dung, devil's dung, devil's dung. It became a rhythmic ostinato accompanying her steps.

The journey from Maryland across Delaware and into Pennsylvania was arduous. Minty trekked most of it during the night by light and guidance of the North Star. She slept during the day. Fortuitously she often found bats' nests to sleep under (which Minty quickly learned would limit the number of mosquito bites she acquired while resting). And, on a few select evenings, she found shelter in a depot or safehouse. The exuberance of escape carried Minty most of the journey. Still, fear and homesickness were constant begrudging companions.

A disheveled and weary Araminta Tubman finally reached Philadelphia on an October day in 1849. Stumbling down the main drag, she was greeted by a bevy of intoxicatingly welcoming and filling sensory experiences, so unlike the sights and smells from her sojourn. Black-skinned vendors roasted oysters whose salty, pungent perfume permeated the air. Others peddled flowers of every color and hue, or matches for fire. Every other corner accommodated roasting chestnuts and corn boiled in its own husk. Buttery, organic, nutty aromas mingled and tantalized while the seaport water's edge alleys buzzed with sail makers, longshoremen and mariners.

A vendor with a shiny, bald head noticed Araminta.

"Hungry?" he asked in a hospitable bass.

Minty nodded sheepishly, "But, I don't have any money." She kicked a pebble.

The smiling vendor ladled some steaming peppery pot into a tin cup. "Take it," he said handing the banquet in a bowl to Araminta. "Looks like you need it more than I do."

Minty inhaled steam that rose from the vegetables and meat stewed with cassava, "Thank you, sir."

"No need to thank me. And, definitely no need to call me sir."

The newcomer smiled at the vendor. She cupped hands 'round the warm fare and walked away, looking for a private spot to sit and sup.

"Hey . . . Missus . . . What's your name?" the kind gentleman called after her.

Two words tickled the tip of Minty's tongue: Araminta Tubman. Before they emerged from her mouth, she stopped walking. Pausing in the middle of the street, her back to the vendor, Araminta struggled for an answer to his simple question, *What's your name?* Hurricanes of thought swirled within her. Sojourner Truth, the new name of freed slave Isabella Baumfree, centered itself in the eye of her hurricane. Araminta wanted to blurt out this poetic appellation or something profound and beautiful like it. In a split second she reasoned the name was too idyllic. *Besides it's already taken*, she thought.

Before Minty realized what she was saying, she turned toward the bald vendor, her shoulders square, back straight as a steal rod, "Harriet Tubman. Name's Harriet Tubman."

"Nice to meet you, Harriet Tubman," said the man, tipping an imaginary hat toward the hungry woman. "I reckon we'll be seeing a lot more of each other 'round these parts."

"I reckon we will," she said and walked away with gratitude as her shadow.

Sitting on a side street several blocks away from the hubbub, Minty savored the stew and her new name. It felt as if something instinctive, visceral, made her choose Harriet, her mother's name. Something loyal, loving, made her keep Tubman. Harriet Tubman. She liked the sound of it, the feel of it. It warmed and invigorated and filled her like the peppery pot.

Harriet couldn't remember a happier day since she'd jumped the broom. Though she was hundreds of miles from Maryland, with each glimpse of the great river, she experienced a deep assurance that it'd be quick and easy to get used to this place. She'd effortlessly fit in. Each smiling passerby affirmed that. Complete strangers felt like brothers and sisters. They extended the kind of welcome one only expects at a family reunion.

On her fifth bite of peppery pot, Harriet tried to recreate the recipe in her mind. *There's parsley and green pepper, carrots, onion, potatoes. I can definitely taste thyme and marjoram, maybe some leeks. But, there's something I'm missing.* She took another bite. Then, another. *What in the world is it? Could it be cloves?* Harriet scraped the last bit from the bowl. She let it linger in her mouth for a moment. *Maybe it's cloves. That's what it might be.* "Cloves," she said aloud as she stood up to start searching for a place to stay that night. Then, taking a deep breath and looking around she thought, *Whatever it is, it tastes like home.*

For about one year Harriet Tubman stayed in Philadelphia working as a laundress and kitchen maid. She saved money, visited public gardens, went to church, frequented cultural institutions, and got to know members of the abolitionist community. Harriet relished her freedom but longed to hear her parents' voices, feel her husband's strong sinewy arms 'round her, to laugh with sisters and brothers.

As autumn winds began to blow, a relentless yearning to return to Maryland and bring her family north overtook Harriet. She had no choice but to acquiesce to its beckoning.

On her first expedition, Harriet freed her niece Kizzy and Kizzy's children. On the second, it was brothers James and Isaac and two strangers. On the third trip, during fall of 1851, Harriet journeyed home to retrieve her husband. It was a devastating blow when she arrived at the Brodess plantation to find John had remarried. This was not a cost she had counted when tabulating the price of freedom.

Bent but not broken, Harriet Tubman leaned into freedom work. She continued her missions, ultimately making more than thirteen sojourns—funded by her own work—to free slaves. Each group traveled by night, tumbling like autumn leaves tossed on the forest floor as if by abolition's tumultuous winds. Harriet's freedom adventures were as daring and dangerous as their leader. She was known to carry a pistol, calm babies with opiates to keep them from crying, and ask her "cargo" to hide in swamps. She was rugged and relentless on the trail. When runaways wanted to quit and return to slavery, Tubman didn't hesitate to wield her gun and threaten, "A live runaway can do lots of harm by going back, but a dead one can tell no secrets."

On one of her traverses betwixt North and South, Harriet and her stowaways were living on the edges of their physical and emotional last nerves. That evening, they had been forced to cross two unapologetically wide, icy, waist-high streams. As dawn broke the ragamuffin crew was cold, wet, fatigued, and fearing capture. They came upon an isolated cabin. Using charm and the power of persuasion, Harriet convinced the impoverished family within to allow her crew to dry off and rest for the day. The cabin's fire warmed their bones, the hostess's victuals satisfied their hunger, conversation fortified their spirits. The travelers devoured a feast of generosity. Bread broken open. A holy commune among them.

Upon their departure the next evening, Harriet didn't have any money to offer the hosts. Creative in her tenacity to give out of nothing, Harriet peeled off some of her garments and gave them to the poor family. On each voyage, Tubman's philanthropic heart beat louder and stronger with undeterred openhandedness, even and limitless out-of-the-box extensions of grace.

Never remiss in giving, Harriet continued her philanthropic ventures even after freeing all of her brothers, sisters, and parents, and serving the Union side in the Civil War. In 1869 when she received news that her first husband, John Tubman, had been murdered, Harriet married Nelson Davis, a man some twenty years her junior and able to keep up with Harriet. Together, Harriet and her new man built the Harriet Tubman Home, a community outreach house, where the couple (and her parents) lived and grew old.

When the house had been finally under roof, the duo started work in the gardens. There were plans for flowers and vegetables. And, along the east side of the house, Harriet planted a long line of apple trees.

Harriet watered holes she'd dug in chocolate-brown soil, then filled them with tiny trees holding the promise of apples. The trees — the anticipated orchard — brought memories. Memories of a day in her adolescence on the Brodess plantation, when the angry overseer whipped her for taking a measly bite out of the harvest. She remembered being whipped again, later that same day, when she was unable to quiet Miss Susan's crying baby boy. She remembered endless nights tumbling in the dark toward Life Set Free. And, she remembered the smiling, bald vendor who'd offered her a comforting bowl of peppery pot on her first day in Philadelphia.

A bumblebee buzzed a circuitous path around Harriet's straw bonnet magically morphing her rememberings into imaginings. She imagined the day her apple trees would yield their first fruit, a particularly round and red crop. On that day, she'd reach toward heaven and pluck a ripe red beauty. Holding it tightly in her hand, she'd walk to the porch and savor each succulent bite in a hapless, casual, yet divine glory. She'd wipe the sweet sticky juice from her chin. Then, standing on her front porch, she'd yell into the cool autumn air and abundance, *"Apples . . . red, juicy apples. Come, take and eat . . . you, who haven't any money, come, buy and eat! Apples, free of charge . . . come pick as many as you want. Fill an entire bushel basket with red, juicy apples. Enjoy and eat what is good and your soul will delight in the richest of fare."*

> *I never met with any person*
> *of any color who had more confidence*
> *in the voice of God,*
> *as spoken direct to*
> *her soul.*
> — Thomas Garrett (about Harriet)

AFTER THE STORY

Harriet Tubman was a paragon of bravery, courage, and determination. She was the first American woman to lead a military operation when she served the Union side during the Civil War. At the Combahee Ferry in June of 1863 Harriet took a heroic part in freeing over 700 slaves.

During her golden years Harriet shared an active, charitable life with Nelson Davis, her new and younger beau. She regularly enchanted audiences with spellbinding tales of her walks along the Liberty Lines. An activist for women's rights, she kowtowed with the likes of Susan B. Anthony. Her love, though, was running the Harriet Tubman Home, which helped freed and runaway slaves and other indigent and homeless. The home still stands in Auburn, New York.

On March 10, 1913, Harriet died. Until the very end, she maintained a philanthropic spirit. On her deathbed, borrowing some of Christ's words as her last, she promised, *"I go to prepare a place for you."* Harriet Tubman was buried in Fort Hill Cemetery with military honors. Numerous accolades followed: in 1944 Eleanor Roosevelt christened a ship the Liberty *Harriet Tubman*, a commemorative postage stamp bore her name and likeness, and in 1994 Freedom Park was created at 17 North Street in Auburn, recognizing her life, memory, and work.

*Moses said to the Lord, "You have been telling me, 'Lead these people,'. . . If you are pleased with me, teach me your ways so I may know you and continue to find favor with you. Remember that this nation is your people."*

*The Lord replied, "My Presence will go with you, and I will give you rest"* (EXODUS 33:12–14 NIV).

CHAPTER 9

# PONDERINGS FOR THE HEART:
## Reflecting on God's Love

Harriet Tubman was a woman who turned tables, swam against the tide, broke chains. Harriet gave what was never given to her. She gave out of nothing. She righted wrongs committed against her by loving, "doing unto others . . ." Harriet, a Maryland slave, freed hundreds of enslaved people. A girl and adolescent deprived of food and material goods; she gave to others with reckless joy and openhandedness, out of her poverty.

Those of us who've been hurt, abused, or neglected can follow in Harriet's footsteps, forging our own liberty lines. Like this heroic woman, we can give to others the very things we were lacking: love, compassion, forgiveness, kind words, money, material belongings, affirmation. Because of Jesus' divine love, we can extend grace, goodness, and help that were never given to us. Following the forged footsteps of women who broke free, we can be part of the redemptive righting of wrongs. Even when we feel resourceless and empty, God's Spirit can show a way of surprising grace . . . that could be as close to us and as unexpected as Harriet's creative garment gifting.

1. Apples played a cameo role in Harriet Tubman's narrative. At first they represented all that she lacked. Later, they were a metaphor for her abundant, overflowing, generous life. Is there an object that represents a way your life is turning around, or a way your life has turned around? A photograph, a song, a tattoo, a memento? Why is that object or iconic image a fitting example of the way God has turned your life around? Share this with a friend, or write in your journal about it.

2. As Harriet prepares to escape from the Brodess plantation, she forfeits saying good-bye to those she loves for their safety and well-being as well as her own. Have you had to forfeit or sacrifice anything important to you in order to be freed from relational, emotional, material, or spiritual bondage? If so, what? Share your answer with a friend. Then, turn the question on her.

3. How do Harriet's consistent encounters with God help you see a divine, loving presence in your own life? Has God spoken words of promise to you the way Harriet received a promise in the apple orchard? She heard God's voice in her mother's words and the words of the Bible. Have you received words of promise or path or purpose from the Scriptures?

4. Harriet gave generously, even in her poverty. She gave freedom, apples, and even her undergarments. Have you been asked to give when you felt like you had figuratively or literally empty pockets? What did you give? How did this giving make you feel? Consider reading Shel Silverstein's classic picture book, *The Giving Tree*. Consider the themes in this tale about a boy and an apple tree in light of Harriet's story, in light of your giving story.

5. What part of Harriet's story reminded you of yourself? Was there anything during her enslaved life in Maryland that magnified an abuse or mistreatment you may have suffered? If so, what specific life experiences came to mind? Could it be an experience in your childhood, goings on in a dysfunctional friendship, or a pattern of relating in your marriage? It can feel extremely tender acknowledging these kinds of hurts. So, be gentle with yourself. Take your time. You may want to talk with a friend, an entrusted group of girlfriends, or even a counselor about memories or feelings you may uncover.

> *Growing from a girl into a young woman, Araminta experienced an intensification of her Christian faith, a deep and abiding spiritual foundation that remained with her throughout her life. Perhaps because she had been so gravely ill during her youth, her mother must have spent as much time as possible by her daughter's sickbed, and naturally filled her head full of Bible stories.*
>
> — CATHERINE CLINTON

# HEARTBEATS:
## Acting on God's Love

1. Listen. Open yourself to the stories of other women. Have any of your friends survived an abusive marriage, a sexual assault, an unhappy childhood? Let their victories be your inspiration, and allow the exuberance of their escape to carry you. Realize that you are surrounded by strong women who want to help. And, when it seems as if it will take forever to get your *Titanic*-type trial turned around — be patient. Give yourself time to heal and rest and be fortified by good friends; food; and long, undefended naps.

2. Hang out with women who share similar wounds. If you're struggling with financial issues, serve your sisters at a soup kitchen or homeless shelter. If you're healing from an abortion, volunteer at a local crisis pregnancy center. Go to a home for abused women if you're feeling hurt or neglected in your own marriage. If you wrestle with physical pain, visit the hospital or nursing home nearest you and ask if you could pray for anyone there. Your help and counsel of others will take you on a freeing adventure. As you share in brokenness with other women, you may find unexpected strength in the sisterhood of humanity.

3. Think of someone who has hurt you. Write them a letter expressing the ways they've caused pain in your life. Then, in the letter, extend words of grace and forgiveness to your offender. Hold onto the letter for as long as you want. When you're ready — if you're ever ready — mail the letter. (Or keep it forever as part of your personal healing journey.)

4. Give yourself time to read and enjoy a passage from Isaiah that inspired part of the chapter about Harriet. Consider Isaiah 55 (*The Message*). You may also want to practice lectio divina: Slowly read the chapter aloud, three times. The first time, listen for a phrase or word that stands out. The second time, reflect on what touches you (share that with a friend or write about it in your journal). Thirdly, respond with a prayer or an act that you feel called to, based on the entire experience. Or more simply: listen, reflect, respond.

# CHAPTER 10

## *My Sacred Love Story*

### THE FACTS

NAME: Sally Miller

DATE OF BIRTH: June 23, Lake Forest, Illinois

DATE OF DEATH: Unknown

OTHERWISE KNOWN AS/NICKNAMES: Sal, Mom, Writer, Sis, Chaplain, Auntie Sal-Sal, Salzy, Sal-Sal

SUMMARY OF YOUR LIFE THUS FAR: I grew up on the North Shore of Lake Michigan in a yellow house nested on a little hill with a walnut tree in the front yard. My childhood was less than perfect, but gave me the gifts of resilience and an ineffably valuable relationship with my brother, Rob. I attended Wheaton College Conservatory and Northwestern University, where I studied music. I also taught music education in the public schools for a decade before meeting my second favorite carpenter, Bryan Miller, who became my husband and the father of our three children. Since becoming a mom, I've begun to write books and speak at women's conferences. I also recently completed work as a seminarian and now serve part-time as a hospital chaplain.

TRIVIA ABOUT ME: I can turn my tongue upside down. My favorite guilty pleasure is watching *The Bachelor*. I love condiments and sauces (barbecue, teriyaki, béarnaise — you name it!). I delight in good music, novels laced with metaphor, my three unique and wondrous children, the bright blue of my husband's eyes.

🙢 NOTABLE: Last time I talked to my brother's wife, Kristin, who I call my sister-in-love, we laughed about calling my sweet and hospitable and humble mom the Self-Deprecating Chef. Also, of note: I would not have made it through this life so far without my dearest friends Cheri, Margie, Heather, Beth, and Jules.

🙢 QUOTABLE: "Red is a neutral." My closest girlfriends like to remind me that I once said this while we were having a conversation about home decor. It seems to point — for them — to the ways my passion and exuberance for living bleeds into the way I see color.

---

A MAXIM OF THE STORY: *All things work out for the good.*

---

Following I share five short personal stories that have become part of my theology, part of the deepest, most meaningful ways I understand God in Christ Jesus. These stories connect me to the women who have been storied in these pages, and more importantly, they connect me to Divine Love. The first story is from my early childhood; the second, third, and fourth occurred a bit later in my life; and the last is a healing story that reminds me of the ways I've reached for God's healing love throughout my spiritual sojourn (much like Maddie).

I share these stories and the action and reflection questions that follow as a seed for you, dear reader. It is my hope that you've seen yourself in the stories of Xiao Min and Harriet and Gomer and Maddie and the others. And maybe you see a thread of their stories in mine? Or, perhaps, a thread of my story in yours? I invite you to write some of your life stories as the final chapter of this book. May that work be a gift and connector, tying you to all of the women's stories that have been recorded here . . . and, most importantly, tying you in to God's epic love story.

## THE TONGUE STORY: *ROB AND I RIP AWAY*

It was January of 1973. My brother, Rob, and I were about five and six years old, respectively. Trees and yard and roofs were covered in the deep, beautiful, icy white wonder that's snow. I remember the day feeling as if it were stuffed full with possibilities of play and mystery and creativity, of friendship and fun, all which were accompanied by a tiny twinge of foreboding danger. Rob and I gathered with neighborhood comrades, most of them our age, but added to the entourage were two nasty high school girls, Robin and Heather.

Together, we constructed a fort in the snow, a castle really: replete with spires and doors and windows, even a drawbridge (if memory serves right). Heather and Robin were the courtiers, taking their places on snowy pillows within the castle. Richie was the court jester. Rob and I, and a few others, were minions. I vaguely remember pretending to be a court horse with my brother. We pattered gloved hands in the snow beside the castle, adding to the drama and majesty: serving the kingdom well.

When the "big girls" got hungry, they cajoled us to have our mom make popcorn, which they devoured, leaving a few measly kernels for us. We were mad for a second. But, we shook it off, running in the drifts, playing in the yard. We threw snowballs and painted snow with spray bottles full of warm food-coloring-dyed water. We made snow angels and snow pies.

It was a glorious day, until . . . Heather and Robin dared my brother and me to go to the bottom of the big hill in our backyard, down by the swing set. Our swing set was huge, and dare I say, ominous looking. It was a swing set that giants could've effectively used. Dad had welded — yes welded — the thing together using black iron rods for the frame. He'd also torn out enormous wooden swing seats from lumber cast offs, and used actual chain — thick and beefy — to hang them. (We got our share of splinters from those seats!) The high school girls glared at our gargantuan swing set, its black rod iron arms and legs glistening from sun and ice.

"We dare you guys to put your tongues on that bar," said the older girl. Rob and I looked at the sisters quizzically.

Jutting out my jaw and crossing my arms at my chest, I asked, "Why?" Though I felt something off in the challenge, I would have been mortified to miss an opportunity for challenge or adventure.

"It's fun. You'll like it," answered Heather. Though I didn't realize it on that ominous day in January, today it's unmitigated that — at that precise moment in history — my bloviating bully smirked in her very soul.

Without much more consideration, and taking the girls at their word, Rob and I — shoulder to shoulder — leaned in toward the Black Iron Beast. We extended our tongues and placed them with full force and exuberance on the nearest frozen crossbar. Instantly, we were stuck like the ubiquitous gum on shoe. Panic and fear mixing with a drop of potent regret coursed through our adrenaline flooded veins. The girls ran up the hill, abandoning us, trailed by echoes of nefarious laughter.

*What are we going to do?* I frenetically worried. For a moment, I tried to call for my mom. But, with tongue adhered to an immovable frozen metropolis and lips soon to follow, I was mute. In an instant, it seemed as if Rob and I had become prehistoric bugs forever trapped in amber. I looked, out of the corner of one wild eye, at my brother. He was petrified into an indescribable stillness. Not knowing what else I could possibly do, I counted to three, then reared back my head like the mustangs I'd read about in *Black Beauty*. Instantly my tender tongue flesh ripped from its frozen grip. Almost immediately, Rob followed.

Together, we ran—wailing—up our backyard hill toward the house. Our tongues hanging out, flailing, blood dripping onto chins, jackets, scarves, and prismatic snow.

# PONDERINGS FOR THE HEART:
## *Reflecting on God's Love*

1. How do you feel, having just read this story?

2. What connections, from your own life, do you make to my story? Are there personal stories my story brings to mind for you?

3. What connections do you make between this story and the stories of biblical, historical, or contemporary women?

4. Where is God in the story?

5. How do your answers to these questions impact your understanding of, or experience of Divine Love?

## A STORY ABOUT THE DEER:
## *ON THE DAY THAT DAD LOVED US*

It was the end of the deer hunting season, winter 1978. I was ten years old. The night, just after dinner, was particularly snowy and dark. I remember watching the snowflakes spiral in the beam of our porch light. My memory is that Mom was in the kitchen. Robbie was in the basement, probably playing a video game. And, I was in my room, with the canopy bed and the blue shag carpet, reading.

When Dad burst in through the front door, I was the first to hear. "I got a deer," he was yelling, out of breath. "He's a ten-point buck!" I flew down the stairs as fast as my brother Robbie and I would sled down the Big Hill on Greenbay Road. Dad's cheeks were ruddy, the color of the Romeo red roses Mom grew on the east side of our little yellow house in Lake Bluff. His eyes sparkled black beneath lacquer-black hair, dotted in snowflakes.

I was the first one in the foyer. The first one to see Dad. The first one to hear his story. The first one to smell the dampness of snow mingling with fresh air on his camouflaged jacket. And the first one to say yes when he asked who wanted to go back to the woods to gut the deer and drag it to the Suburban.

Robbie wanted to go too. And, for a second, as he laced up his boots, I wondered if this was going to be a men-only trip or if I would be included too. Nonchalantly, as if I didn't care if I stayed home or went on the adventure, I laced up my boots. Hiding my glee and expectation, I put on my coat and the extra-long, striped hat-and-scarf-in-one fashion statement that Mom had knit for me that winter. I'll never forget that orange and brown and pink and red atrocious work of art: my favorite gift of the season. Robbie made fun of it. It embarrassed him when I wore that "hat thing" (said with malice and hatred) to school. But, what really set him off was when I'd wear my *Jesus Loves You* pin, stuck to the front of my jean jacket.

The three of us got into the car. I didn't mention my suspicious fear that I might not actually be invited. I also made a conscious decision not to question why Mom wasn't coming with us, for fear of any drama that might derail the adventure.

On the way to the woods, Dad and Rob talked about the thrill of the hunt: the conquest. They laughed about the way Dad had taught Robbie — when they used to sit in deer stands awaiting the prey — to turn the bill of his hat in the direction of any approaching deer, a tried and true signal of fresh meat. I sat in the back seat, glad to be along — but definitely in my own world — daydreaming, pressing my cheek against the cold car window so I could look deeply into the blue-black night, in order to make pictures out of my favorite constellations.

The deer was "bedded down" at the bottom of a hill, at least three miles from where Dad had to park. We trudged through fresh snow to the fresh kill. I don't know why, but as we knelt beside the beast, I was surprised at the amount of warmth still radiating from the newly dead creature. I took off my glove and stroked the soft, still warm coat. My dad flipped over the buck and told us that he was about to dress the animal.

In quick, skilled and methodical cuts, my dad opened the abdominal cavity. A burst of steam from the body — and something I imagined as animal *spirit* — floated into the air. One organ at a time, my father eviscerated the deer. Dad identified the organs, and I reveled at naming each of them aloud: *liver, heart, large intestine, small intestine*. This was an archetypal science class dissection experiment. But, we were not in a classroom. We were in the school of real life!

Dad told us stories of Native Americans and buffalo as he worked adeptly with knife and bare, blood-covered hands. I remember imagining my dad as a native, feathered and with buckskin clothes. The imagery made perfect sense knowing Dad's wise ways in nature.

As I knelt in the snow, I noticed crimson splotches on the icy white. I felt sad at the loss of this animal's life. Simultaneously, I was rapt with fascination as I watched each organ emerge looking like a soft, shiny jewel, each an enormous ruby covered in sparkling blood.

Once the deer was disemboweled, Dad trussed the animal's legs in pairs so that we could drag it up the hill and back to the Suburban. I remember the joy of feeling like I was really helping; I was necessary and part of this utilitarian team. It felt good to work hard, to work together, to exert my body and breathe deeply of cold fresh air. There was a joy and aliveness in seeing translucent-white proof of our being (our breath), hearing our feet work together for a purpose and with a plan.

The first mile, Dad listed all of the cuts of meat he would have the butcher prepare: venison steaks, venison burgers, sausage, ground venison, and so on. Though this was repulsive to me, knowing that hours before this buck ran wild in the woods, I felt better somehow knowing that the life of this beautiful beast would give food and life to our family.

Halfway up the hill, the three of us became breathless, our muscles began to fatigue and even cramp at the calves. "Let's take a break," Dad said, turning his back to the hill and falling, as if into a feather bed, onto the snowy hill. Robbie and I mimicked. The three of us lay in the deep, soft snow looking up at the infinite sky. It was a stellar glory like I had never seen: a Braille-like cacophony of light and darkness. Our breath, our intentions, our lives unified in a moment of mystical — almost primordial — ontological togetherness.

In that moment my dad was happy. I felt like he deeply loved Rob and me, and his life with us. I felt like I was part of his life and part of a meaningful moment of learning and discovery and family and beauty and peace. The moment was one of those magic moments that seems frozen in time, the stuff that's in books and poems and plays, and maybe only happens once or twice in one's childhood.

# PONDERINGS FOR THE HEART:
## *Reflecting on God's Love*

1. How do you feel, having just read this story?

2. What connections, from your own life, do you make to my story? Are there personal stories my story brings to mind for you?

3. What connections do you make between this story and the stories of historical, biblical, or contemporary women?

4. Where is God in the story?

5. How do your answers to these questions impact your understanding of, or experience of, Divine Love?

## THE STORY ABOUT THE BOYS AND ME:
### *A FEW GLORIOUS HOURS*

At Grandma Norberg's, in Mankato, Minnesota, I am the only girl in a world of boys. There is Robbie, my brother. And there are my cousins, Tuggy and Jimmy. Even Bowser, the sky-black Gordon setter with ancient feathers and a howling-moan, which sounds distinctly human, is a boy. Sadly, like the little boys, even Bowser does not enjoy nor tolerate my love of art and drama, my propensity for life's little vagaries. At least he talks to me at night when we sleep together under the ironed and starched pink and white striped sheets in Grandma's pull out bed in the basement. On most visits, Bowser is my only companion.

The boys are always busy with each other, partaking of quotidian dances, which, typically beginning with wrestling, transition into basketball on the driveway, and inevitably end at the dock with fishing rods and earthworms specked with tiny dots of fresh dirt. The trinity of boys is easily amused with the common routines, the expected ebbs and flows of each day.

I, on the contrary, want meaning and creativity, some kind of extraordinary event to mark the moments. I want music and color. I want giddiness and miracles and tornadic adventure. So I try to draw the boys in to my world. Like a spiritual director, I try drawing them in: "Boys, come downstairs. I have a play for you all to star in. We can play the music on Grandpa's jukebox. You can be KISS. I have parts for each of you . . . costumes . . . dance moves . . . lines . . ."

At first the boys are intrigued, hooked like their little Sunfish off the dock. They agree to the all black-and-white outfits. They sit in folding chairs for at least thirty minutes each while I apply whiteface, accented by black stars, lightning bolts, and spirals. They learn my lip-sync, including the air-guitar and drum solo moves.

For a few glorious hours, I am the choreographer, the director, the mastermind and genesis of all things fabulous and fun. At one point in the rehearsal, perhaps when I arranged the boys in a frozen tableau, Robbie says, "You're being way too bossy, Sal. We just wanna go outside." Jimmy and Tug agree.

They all begin to get squirmy and resistant to my suggestions to continue the rehearsal, "for just a few more minutes . . . and then we'll be ready to show our masterpiece to the grown-ups: to Mom and Dad, and Grandma and Grandpa, and Auntie Cristie!"

I try being nice. I use my saccharine voice and let them be part of the plan by adding their stupid awkward dance moves to the routine. They're over it. Like water irrevocably slipping through the cracks in my hands, they leave the basement, wiping off makeup, leaving a trail of costumes and props in piles on the cement floor. I sit amidst the mess wondering what I could have done differently. I hear the basketball bouncing buoyantly on the driveway. I wish there was someone in my family who was like me, alive with possibility and imagination.

## PONDERINGS FOR THE HEART:
### *Reflecting on God's Love*

1. How do you feel, having just read this story?

2. What connections, from your own life, do you make to my story? Are their personal stories my story brings to mind for you?

3. What connections do you make between this story and the stories of historical, biblical, or contemporary women?

4. Where is God in the story?

5. How do your answers to these questions impact your understanding of, or experience of, Divine Love?

## THE STORY ABOUT SISTER ANITA:
## SITTING ON THE PIANO BENCH

Sister Anita is visiting our home in Lake Bluff. At the time, I wanted to be a nun when I grew up. So, when a real-live nun was coming to our house for spaghetti and meatballs and banana cream pie, I thought I might burst out of my skin. Anita went to Faribault, Minnesota's, parochial school, Bethlehem Academy, with my dad years ago. I wondered if she'd wear her habit for the visit. I also wondered if Anita had surreptitiously held on to a burning crush on my dad for all these years.

I imagined how this visit might break up my parent's marriage. And, I imagined how this seemingly innocent dinner could potentially cause Sister Anita to leave the convent. *Would she, then, have to divorce God?* I contemplated every permutation of the possibilities.

Once Sister Anita arrived, none of that mattered, though. I was completely mesmerized and enchanted by her. She was tall and dark-haired, like me. She wore light blue polyester pants and a matching print blouse. She was pretty, though she didn't wear but a scant trace of makeup (pinkish cheeks and a dab of scented lip gloss). Anita was round, kind of padded, unlike my overly skinny mother. And Anita had soft, meaty hands, which I could not stop admiring.

I felt drawn to Sister Anita as if I were a moth and she, a diadem, was circled by an aura of radiant light, a halo, a wreath of sunbeam. Almost immediately, Anita began paying attention to me, asking me questions about school and music and life as a little girl. Anita had come to visit my dad. But, if I hadn't been told that, I would have thought she came to meet me.

After dinner, the nun led me to the living room, where she asked me to sit beside her on the piano bench before the upright piano. With grace and little effort, and with those soft, milky hands, she played a song—in two parts—for me. Within moments, she taught me the easier of the two parts. And, in a sacred moment where I felt simultaneously beautiful and utilitarian, we created art together:

playing the duet. When the song ended and the coffee pot was empty, I wished Anita would never leave.

After she did go, I played her melody over and over until it drove everyone in my family crazy. Every time I played that simple, yet miraculous tune, I got a little catch in my throat because it conjured feelings of being loved and companioned, mentored, and seen. The notes beneath my fingers and in my ears reminded me of Anita, and I knew that — someday — I wanted to be just like her.

# PONDERINGS FOR THE HEART:
## *Reflecting on God's Love*

1. How do you feel, having just read this story?

2. What connections, from your own life, do you make to my story? Are there personal stories my story brings to mind for you?

3. What connections do you make between this story and the stories of historical, biblical, or contemporary women?

4. Where is God in the story?

5. How do your answers to these questions impact your understanding of, or experience of, Divine Love?

## A HEALING STORY:
### *THE DAY TWO WOMEN PRAYED FOR ME*

Excruciating, debilitating, chronic back pain led me to doctors, surgeons, and ultimately to a little church, Church of the Great Shepherd, pastored by Lyle Dorsett, that offers healing prayers for anyone who is broken like me. Lay ministers at Great Shepherd offer healing prayer during Sunday services as part of the worship. These ministers listen to the stories of the broken, lay on hands, and often offer words or images (they call these "pictures") from the divine. (One of my dear friends from Wheaton College—who is a healing prayer minister—differentiates healing prayer from intercession with the nomenclature *Presence Prayer*): it is the kind of prayer in which listening supersedes speaking. And, the voice of God provides the prominent portion of the dialogue.

It was Advent 2002. I had been interceded for by elders and friends and family members. But the nefarious pain would not relent. In a last ditch effort to remit the suffering, I attended a service at Great Shepherd. After the sermon, while worship music filled the sanctuary, I approached two female prayer ministers who stood on the side of the sanctuary. In tears, I told them that I had been suffering from excruciating back pain since the birth of my sons. Both women laid hands on me and prayed.

Honestly, I can't remember any of their words. (On second thought, there might have been something about uneven lengths of my legs? And asking God to grow the shorter one. I remember thinking that was kind of strange, and that I became preoccupied with hunger that led to thoughts of an afterchurch cheeseburger.) At one point during the prayer, my arms began involuntarily moving. *What is going on?* I wondered. I tried to ignore the bizarre phenomenon until one of the women asked if I was moving my arms. It was comforting that she noticed, and did not seem alarmed (as if she'd experienced this unsolicited undulation before). I answered, "No. I'm not moving my arms." At this point, my eyes were open and I was looking down at my active appendages as if they were dismembered members of myself with wild wills of their own.

The prayer minister knowingly nodded and with an unswerving fortitude continued to pray as if I wasn't the spiritual pariah or freak that I felt I was. I don't remember a whole lot more except that I had a deeply intuitive sense of *knowing* that I had experienced a measure of God's mysterious, ineffable healing.

As I was about to leave the prayer aisle, the older of the two prayers said, "I have a word from the Lord for you." I remember thinking, *Great! Now comes the shame* . . . I braced myself for words of *should* and *why did you?* And *I condemn you to blah, blah, blah.* Surreptitiously she whispered in my ear, "Just remember to say thanks."

I inhaled deeply. I could still feel the familiar ache in my back. But, in that moment, I felt as clarified and warm as morning sunshine beaming through my kitchen window. I walked out to my car wondering what had just happened. Under my breath and probably 100 times (or more), I said, "Thank You, thank You, thank You, thank You . . ."

## PONDERINGS FOR THE HEART:
### *Reflecting on God's Love*

1. How do you feel, having just read this story?

2. What connections, from your own life, do you make to my story? Are there personal stories my story brings to mind for you?

3. What connections do you make between this story and the stories of historical, biblical, or contemporary women?

4. Where is God in the story?

5. How do your answers to these questions impact your understanding of, or experience of, Divine Love?

Today, I'm a wife to Bryan, a mother to two biological boys, Ben (14) and Ayden (12), and to a little girl adopted from China, Emily (9). While my family is the delight of my life, during this season of mothering older kids who are becoming busy with their own lives and dreams, I regularly find myself serving at a nearby hospital as a chaplain. I also write and speak at women's gatherings, when time allows.

Daily, I carry the stories of Maddie and Endora, Pocahontas, and and all of God's beloved women featured in these writings. They are with me in deeply ontological ways, wherever I go. They remind me to follow a greater wisdom, take risks to accept the challenges of life's great absurdities, to die before I die, and, most profoundly, to remember that I, too, am a Beloved Woman. Parts of my story intersect with their stories and pieces of their stories will remain with me, in me, always.

Now, it is my hope to add your stories to the intermingling of words and ideas, themes and characters, epiphanies, and adventures. It is my hope that you will see yourself and your friends in the stories of these women as they reach for Divine Love, wait for it, hope for it, believe in it, and live out their dreams because of it. It is my ultimate dream that ways of connecting with God's perfect, mind-blowing love, will inspire you to taste and touch and experience love that makes your life meaningful and rich . . . a love that is wider and deeper and higher than you could've ever hoped for or imagined!

# CHAPTER 11

## *Your Sacred Love Story*

### THE FACTS

NAME:

DATE OF BIRTH:

DATE OF DEATH: Unknown

OTHERWISE KNOWN AS/NICKNAMES:

🙰 SUMMARY OF YOUR LIFE THUS FAR:

🙰 TRIVIA ABOUT YOU:

🙰 NOTABLE:

🙰 QUOTABLE:

# A Maxim of the Story:

## THE STORY

Start to write your life story . . . continue it in a journal.

AFTER THE STORY
YOUR HOPES FOR THE FUTURE

Write a continuation of your life story including hopes and dreams and ways you want to encounter God's love in your daily life . . .

## PONDERINGS FOR THE HEART:
### *Reflecting on God's Love*

Consider summarizing themes and main ideas that have come forth in the writing of your life story. Perhaps write questions for reflection and actions that may dawn on you as you reflect.

Or, if you gather in a group to share your stories, feel free to use my questions (which are based on a story theology model). They're the questions I used in my sacred love story, which you'll find in the previous chapter. But, I'll include them below for you to use with your own stories, as well.

1.

2.

3.

4.

# HEARTBEATS:
## *Acting on God's Love*

1.

2.

3.

PONDERINGS FOR THE HEART:
*Reflecting on God's Love*

1. How do you feel, having just read this story?

2. What connections, from your own life, do you make to my story? Are there personal stories my story brings to mind for you?

3. What connections do you make between this story and the stories of historical, biblical, or contemporary women?

4. Where is God in the story?

5. How do your answers to these questions impact your understanding of, or experience of, Divine Love?

Dearest Reader:

I offer blessings on you as you continue to reflect on the lives of these women. I truly hope you'll consider recording your own sacred love story, or parts of it.

I hope this writing becomes a gift to yourself and to others. If you take time to record your own story and would like share it with me; I would be honored. You can contact me at sallypmiller@gmail.com or via thewordgirls.com.

Thank for reading my words. I wait, in eager expectation, to read some of yours.

May you continue to experience Divine Love in every corner of your life,

Sally Miller

*And I ask God, that with both feet planted firmly on love,
you'll be able to take in with all followers of Jesus the
extravagant dimensions of Christ's love. Reach out and
experience the breadth! Test its length! Plumb the depths!
Rise to the heights! Live full lives, full in the fullness of God.*
— EPHESIANS 3:17–19 *(The Message)*

# For Further Reading . . . Some Love Notes

CHAPTER 1, GOMER SEES HERSELF IN THE EYES OF LOVE

Hebrew Bible: Book of Hosea, especially chapters 1–3.

Butler, Trent C., *Holman Bible Dictionary* (Nashville: Holman Bible Publishers, 1991), 138.

Michael Card cut titled, "Song of Gomer": http://www.youtube.com/watch?v=IhvLFY89sPw

CHAPTER 2, THE WOMAN OF BLEEDING REACHES OUT

The Bible: Matthew 9:18–23; Mark 5:25–34; Luke 8:43–48

Ann Spangler & Jean E. Syswerda, *Women of the Bible* (Grand Rapids: Zondervan, 1999), 333–40.

CHAPTER 3, DORCAS DIES BEFORE SHE DIES

The Bible: Acts 9:36–42.
http://en.wikipedia.org/wiki/Dorcas_Society

CHAPTER 4, THE WOMAN OF ENDOR REACHES FOR LIFE

Hebrew Bible: Book of 1 Samuel, chapter 28.

Ann Spangler & Jean E. Syswerda, *Women of the Bible* (Grand Rapids: Zondervan, 1999), 168–74.

CHAPTER 5, SONG LISTENS TO THE MELODY OF GOD

http://video.google.com/videoplay?docid=-6923892750736776389

http://www.chinasoul.com/e/cross/script4.htm

CHAPTER 6, JOAN OF ARC'S GREAT ABSURDITY

Mary Gordon, *Joan of Arc* (New York: Viking Penguin, 2000).

Edward Lucie-Smith, *Joan of Arc* (New York: W. W. Norton, 1977).

Régine Pernoud, *Joan of Arc: Her Story* (New York: St. Martins Press, 1998).

Willard Trask, *Joan of Arc: In Her Own Words* (New York: BOOKS & Co., 1996).

http://archive.joan-of-arc.org/index.html

David Hazard, *I Promise You a Crown: A 40-Day Journey in the Company of Julian of Norwich* (Minneapolis: Bethany House Publishers, 1995).

Sheila Upjohn, *In Search of Julian of Norwich* (Grand Rapids: Eerdmans Publishing Company, 1996).

Sheila Upjohn, *Why Julian Now? A Voyage of Discovery* (Grand Rapids: Eerdmans Publishing Company, 1997).

http://www.luminarium.org/medlit/julian.htm

CHAPTER 7, JULIAN OF NORWICH IMAGINES BEYOND HERSELF

Monica Furlong, *Visions and Longings: Medieval Women Mystics* (Boston: Shambhala, 1996), 186–247.

## CHAPTER 8, POCAHONTAS DREAMS GOD'S DREAMS

Allen, Paula Gunn, *Pocahontas: Medicine Woman, Spy, Entrepreneur, Diplomat* (New York: HarperSanFransisco, 2003).

*Pocahontas Revealed: Science Examines an American Legend* as seen on NOVA; may be ordered through Public Television 1-800-949-8670.

Books on Tape, *Pocahontas: My Own Story* by Captain John Smith, available by calling 1-800-88-BOOKS, Book Number 3781.


## CHAPTER 9, HARRIET GIVES A GRACE OUT OF NOTHING

Sarah Bradford, *Harriet Tubman, the Moses of Her People* (1886; reprint, Bedford, MA: Applewood Books, 1993).

Catherine Clinton, *Harriet Tubman: The Road to Freedom* (New York: Little, Brown and Company, 2005).

Jean M. Humez, *Harriet Tubman: The Life and the Life Stories* (Madison: The University of Wisconsin Press, 2004).

Glennette Tilley Turner, *An Apple for Harriet Tubman* (Morton Grove: Albert Whitman & Company, 2006).

Kate Clifford Larson, *Bound for the Promised Land: Harriet Tubman: Portrait of an American Hero* (New York: Ballantine Books, 2004).

www.harriettubman.com

Harriet Beecher Stowe, *Uncle Tom's Cabin*

WorldCrafts℠ develops sustainable, fair-trade businesses among impoverished people around the world. Each WorldCrafts product represents lives changed by the opportunity to earn an income with dignity and to hear the offer of everlasting life.

Visit WorldCrafts.org to learn more about WorldCrafts artisans, hosting WorldCrafts parties and to shop!

# WORLDCRAFTS℠
## Committed. Holistic. Fair Trade.
WorldCrafts.org  1-800-968-7301

WorldCrafts is a division of WMU®.

New Hope® Publishers is a division of WMU®, an international organization that challenges Christian believers to understand and be radically involved in God's mission. For more information about WMU, go to wmu.com. More information about New Hope books may be found at NewHopeDigital.com. New Hope books may be purchased at your local bookstore.

Find additional resources at:

Use the QR reader on your smartphone to visit us online at NewHopeDigital.com

If you've been blessed by this book, we would like to hear your story. The publisher and author welcome your comments and suggestions at: newhopereader@wmu.org.

# Bible Study On the Go!

## Interact. Engage. Grow.

New Hope Interactive is a new digital Bible study platform that allows you to unlock content to download your favorite New Hope Bible study workbooks on your tablet or mobile device. Your answers and notes are kept private through a profile that's easy to create and FREE!

**Perfect for individual or small group use!**

To learn more visit NewHopeInteractive.com/getstarted